Tom Pendergast
& Sara Pendergast,
Editors

Detroit • New York • San Diego • San Francisco • Cleveland • New Haven, Conn. • Waterville, Maine • London • Munich

U•X•L American Decades, 1910–1919

Tom Pendergast and Sara Pendergast, Editors

Project Editors
Diane Sawinski, Julie L. Carnagie, and Christine Slovey

Editorial
Elizabeth Anderson

Permissions
Shalice Shah-Caldwell

Imaging and Multimedia
Dean Dauphinais

Product Design
Pamela A.E. Galbreath

Composition
Evi Seoud

Manufacturing
Rita Wimberley

For permission to use material from this product, submit your request via Web at http://www.gale-edit.com/permissions, or you may download our Permissions Request form and submit your request by fax or mail to:

Permissions Department
The Gale Group, Inc.
27500 Drake Rd.
Farmington Hills, MI 48331-3535
Permissions Hotline:
248-699-8006 or 800-877-4253, ext. 8006
Fax: 248-699-8074 or 800-762-4058

Cover photograph reproduced by permission of the Corbis Corporation.

While every effort has been made to ensure the reliability of the information presented in this publication, The Gale Group, Inc. does not guarantee the accuracy of the data contained herein. The Gale Group, Inc. accepts no payment for listing; and inclusion in the publication of any organization, agency, institution, publication, service, or individual does not imply endorsement of the editors or publisher. Errors brought to the attention of the publisher and verified to the satisfaction of the publisher will be corrected in future editions.

Vol. 1: 0-7876-6455-3
Vol. 2: 0-7876-6456-1
Vol. 3: 0-7876-6457-X
Vol. 4: 0-7876-6458-8
Vol. 5: 0-7876-6459-6
Vol. 6: 0-7876-6460-X
Vol. 7: 0-7876-6461-8
Vol. 8: 0-7876-6462-6
Vol. 9: 0-7876-6463-4
Vol. 10: 0-7876-6464-2

LIBRARY OF CONGRESS CATALOGING-IN-PUBLICATION DATA

U•X•L American decades
   p. cm.
Includes bibliographical references and index.
   Contents: v. 1. 1900-1910—v. 2. 1910-1919—v. 3.1920-1929—v. 4. 1930-1939—v. 5. 1940-1949—v. 6. 1950-1959—v. 7. 1960-1969—v. 8. 1970-1979—v. 9.1980-1989—v. 10. 1990-1999.
   Summary: A ten-volume overview of the twentieth century which explores such topics as the arts, economy, education, government, politics, fashions, health, science, technology, and sports which characterize each decade.
   ISBN 0-7876-6454-5 (set: hardcover: alk. paper)
   1. United States—Civilization—20th century—Juvenile literature. 2. United States—History—20th century—Juvenile literature. [1. United States—Civilization—20th century. 2. United States—History—20th century.] I. UXL (Firm) II. Title: UXL American decades. III. Title: American decades.
E169.1.U88 2003
973.91—dc21
   2002010176

Contents

Reader's Guide

U•X•L American Decades provides a broad overview of the major events and people that helped to shape American society throughout the twentieth century. Each volume in this ten-volume set chronicles a single decade and begins with an introduction to that decade and a timeline of major events in twentieth-century America. Following are eight chapters devoted to these categories of American endeavor:

- Arts and Entertainment
- Business and the Economy
- Education
- Government, Politics, and Law
- Lifestyles and Social Trends
- Medicine and Health
- Science and Technology
- Sports

These chapters are then divided into five sections:

Chronology: A timeline of significant events within the chapter's particular field.

Overview: A summary of the events and people detailed in that chapter.

Headline Makers: Short biographical accounts of key people and their achievements during the decade.

❖ **Topics in the News:** A series of short topical essays describing events and people within the chapter's theme.

✛ **For More Information:** A section that lists books and Web sites directing the student to further information about the events and people covered in the chapter.

OTHER FEATURES

Each volume of *U•X•L American Decades* contains more than eighty black-and-white photographs and illustrations that bring the events and people discussed to life and sidebar boxes that expand on items of high interest to readers. Concluding each volume is a general bibliography of books and Web sites that explore the particular decade in general and a thorough subject index that allows readers to easily locate the events, people, and places discussed throughout that volume of *U•X•L American Decades*.

ACKNOWLEDGMENTS

The editor would like to offer thanks to many people for their help and support during the writing of this book. The series editors, Tom and Sara Pendergast have, as always, been supportive, encouraging, and critical in just the right amounts. James Yardley at <www.ask-a-librarian.org.uk> and Gail Keutzer at the Internet Public Library <www.ipl.org> were extremely helpful with difficult-to-find dates and obscure facts. Thanks to Esme Miskimmin for keeping the editor entertained with tea breaks during long days in the library at the University of Liverpool. And the editor would like to offer thanks to his wife, Siobhan, for putting up with lectures on whatever aspect of American history had been the obsession for the day, and a lot more besides.

COMMENTS AND SUGGESTIONS

We welcome your comments on *U•X•L American Decades* and suggestions for other history topics to consider. Please write: Editors, *U•X•L American Decades,* U•X•L, 27500 Drake Rd., Farmington Hills, MI 48331-3535; call toll-free: 1-800-877-4253; fax: 248-699-8097; or send e-mail via http://www.galegroup.com

Chronology of the 1910s

1910: Electric washing machines become popular in American homes.

1910: **March 26** Congress amends the Immigration Act of 1907, prohibiting criminals, anarchists, the poor, and people carrying infectious diseases from entering the United States.

1911: **March 25** A fire at the Triangle Shirtwaist Factory on New York City's Lower East Side results in the death of 146 female workers.

1911: **May 15** The Supreme Court rules that Standard Oil Company of New Jersey must be dissolved under antitrust laws.

1911: **May 30** Ray Harroun wins the first-ever Indianapolis 500 auto race.

1911: **August 8** *Pathe's Weekly,* the first regular newsreel to be produced in the United States, is released to motion picture theaters.

1912: French-born surgeon Alexis Carrel is the first American to win the Nobel Prize in medicine for suturing, or tying together, blood vessels.

1912: **April 20** Fenway Park, home of baseball's Boston Red Sox, opens.

1913: Henry Ford introduces the assembly line, employed in the manufacturing of automobiles.

1913: The American Cancer Society is organized.

1913: Mammography, an X-ray process for detecting breast cancer, is developed.

1913: The completion of the Panama Canal marks an opportunity for new trade possibilities between Atlantic and Pacific nations.

1913: The major league New York Highlanders are rechristened the Yankees.

1913: **February 25** The Sixteenth Amendment is adopted, legalizing a federal income tax.

1913: **December 23** The Federal Reserve System is established by the Federal Reserve Act to provide stable banking policies for the nation.

1914: The Mayo family opens its Mayo Clinic building in Rochester, Minnesota.

1914: **March** Comedian Charles Chaplin begins to develop the legendary character of the Little Tramp in the film *Mabel's Strange Predicament.*

1915: German-born physicist Albert Einstein discloses his general theory of relativity.

1915: The Victor Talking Machine company introduces a record player called the Victrola.

1915: Modern dancers Ruth St. Denis and Ted Shawn found the Denishawn School of Dancing in Los Angeles.

1915: **January 15** The first transcontinental telephone line becomes available for service between New York City and San Francisco.

1915: **December 10** The one-millionth Model T automobile rolls off the assembly line at the Ford Motor Company's Highland Park, Michigan, plant.

1916: An epidemic of polio (a viral infection which results in fever, paralysis, and muscle atrophy) breaks out, striking more than twenty-eight thousand victims. Six thousand die, and many more are permanently crippled.

1916: The practice of refrigerating blood for transfusions is instituted.

1916: Margaret Sanger, a prominent advocate of birth control, is found guilty of obscenity charges in New York State for distributing her 1914 book *Family Limitation.*

1916: The American Federation of Teachers (AFT), a teacher-only labor union of the American Federation of Labor (AFL), is founded with John Dewey's assistance.

1916: Boeing Aircraft designs and produces its first model, a biplane.

1916: **February 7** An organizing committee establishes the Professional Golfer's Association (PGA). Two months later, the first-ever PGA golf tournament is held.

1916: **November** Lee De Forest begins to transmit daily music broadcasts from his home in New York City.

1917: **April 6** The United States enters World War I.

1917: **May 18** The Selective Service Act passes, which authorizes federal conscription (the draft) and requires male U.S. citizens aged twenty-one to thirty to register for enrollment in the military.

1917: **November 6** An amendment to the New York State constitution gives women the right to vote in state elections.

1918: The nation's first three-color traffic light (red, amber, green) is installed in New York City.

1918: A toy company in New York City starts manufacturing Raggedy Ann dolls. Soon the production grows into a $20 million-per-year business.

1918: **April 8** The National War Labor Board is set up to settle labor disputes in order to avoid disrupting war production.

1918: **June 14** On Flag Day, "Americanization" meetings are held, urging the need to educate recent immigrants in American language, citizenship, and ideals.

1918: **August 27** The "Spanish" influenza epidemic begins in the United States with the diagnosis of two sailors in Boston.

1919: Sir Barton becomes the first racehorse to win the Triple Crown.

1919: **January 29** The Eighteenth Amendment, which prohibited the transportation and sale of alcoholic beverages, is ratified by Congress.

1919: **February 5** United Artists, an independent film distribution company, is founded by Charles Chaplin, Douglas Fairbanks, D.W. Griffith, and Mary Pickford.

1919: **October** The Radio Corporation of America (RCA) is founded.

1919: October Several members of the Chicago White Sox throw the World Series.

1919: November 19 The U.S. Senate fails to ratify the Treaty of Versailles ending World War I, making membership in the newly established League of Nations all but impossible.

The 1910s: An Overview

Powerful social and economic changes occurred in the United States during the 1910s. As the decade began, America was the wealthiest nation in the world. Faced with the prospect of joining a bloody international conflict when World War I (1914–18) broke out in Europe, the United States tried to maintain a neutral stance. Finally, the country was compelled to enter the conflict in 1917. Millions of American men entered the military. Thousands were wounded or killed in battle. The war had a tremendous impact on the country. Economically, the United States grew even wealthier by selling food and supplies to Europe. Politically and socially, the war caused America to grow from an isolationist nation to a world power. By the end of the decade, the United States was as rich as most European countries combined. However, it had learned the hard lessons of war, which included loss of life and a loss of innocence.

Live theater was popular. Vaudeville and musical revues featured songs penned by Tin Pan Alley composers. Dramas remained traditional, but a young playwright named Eugene O'Neill (1888–1953) was beginning to write psychological plays that analyzed the human condition. Novelists captured American life, and the motion picture business blossomed, with feature-length films coming to dominate the industry. Film studios migrated from the East Coast to the West Coast, with many taking root among the rural orange groves of Hollywood, California. Producers began identifying by name the actors in their films, giving birth to the concept of the "movie star."

To keep up with the growing demands of big business and industry, the decade saw the rise of the modern factory and assembly line. As many more jobs became available in the cities, Americans moved from rural areas to crowded urban centers. Instead of working on farms or in small stores or mills, laborers were finding jobs in massive industrial plants, in which they earned higher salaries. Workers joined labor unions to ensure that their wages were maintained and increased and that their hours and working conditions were humane. Where there were problems, workers went on strike. Meanwhile, as jobs became more dependent upon machinery, many in the labor force became dehumanized, little more than drudges and cogs in assembly lines.

Racial and gender discrimination also prevailed in all aspects of society. At the time, women had not yet been granted the right to vote. African Americans struggled to attain equality, but their civil rights often were denied them through a system of "Jim Crow" laws by which white southerners called for separate restrooms, schools, theaters, and water fountains for blacks. Waves of immigrants, mostly from European nations, were settling in the United States. They generally were viewed with distrust by the mainstream population.

The 1918 election saw the Republican Party take control of the U.S. Congress. Party politics stifled the postwar international peace initiatives of Democratic President Woodrow Wilson (1856–1924) in the United States. Then in 1919, the Eighteenth Amendment of the U.S. Constitution was ratified, prohibiting the production, transportation, and sale of alcoholic beverages. Prohibition soon split the country into political and moral factions, and created a powerful and destructive underground culture of bootleg liquor that helped characterized the 1920s.

The new city-centered lifestyle led Americans, particularly the young, to become more fashion and lifestyle conscious. Women in particular became active consumers, shopping for everything from evening dresses to apple peelers in small chain stores or huge urban department stores and through mail-order catalogs. The new consumer culture was spurred on by a fast-growing advertising industry that presented products such as automobiles, iceboxes, and hand cream as keys to success. As the economy changed, secondary school students began taking courses in vocational subjects, which better prepared them for life in the new industrial workplace. A movement in progressive education led to encouraging students to develop as good citizens. Yet public schools in areas of the country, and particularly in the South, remained impoverished.

A surge of technical advances excited public interest. Airplane distance and speed records were established. Synthetic plastic was invented. New uses for electricity were uncovered. The link between food content and disease was acknowledged. American arts were experiencing a rebirth as artists and writers moved away from European inspirations and towards art movements inspired by American lifestyles. In the sports world, the 1910s was a decade of firsts. The Indianapolis 500 debuted, the Professional Golf's Association (PGA) was established, and women's competitions were added to the Olympic Games. Changes introduced in the 1910s would have an impact on the rest of the century.

Arts and Entertainment

1910: **February 28** Russian ballerina Anna Pavlova makes her American debut at the Metropolitan Opera House in New York City.

1910: **March 28** The first one-man show by artist Pablo Picasso opens at the 291 Gallery in New York City.

1910: **November 3** The Chicago Grand Opera opens with a production of *Aida,* by Giuseppe Verdi.

1911: Irving Berlin composes "Alexander's Ragtime Band," the song that popularized ragtime music.

1911: **May 23** President William Howard Taft dedicates the New York Public Library.

1911: **August 8** *Pathe's Weekly,* the first regular newsreel to be produced in the United States, is released to motion picture theaters.

1911: **December 19** The Association of American Painters and Sculptors is founded.

1912: **August** Photographer and editor Alfred Stieglitz devotes an entire issue of his periodical *Camera Work* to the modern art movement.

1912: **October 31** *The Musketeers of Pig Alley,* a film by D. W. Griffith that points out the social evils of poverty and crime on the streets of New York, is released.

1912: **December 10** The Famous Players Film Company registers for copyright the five-reel feature film *The Count of Monte Cristo,* directed by Edwin S. Porter, with James O'Neill recreating his famous stage role.

1913: The Jesse Lasky Feature Play Company, which later would become Paramount Pictures, is established in Hollywood, California.

1913: **February 17** The International Exhibition of Modern Art, known as The Armory Show, opens in New York City. It is the first opportunity for many Americans to view modern art.

1913: **March 24** The million dollar, eighteen-hundred-seat Palace Theatre opens in New York City.

1914: **February 13** The American Society of Composers, Authors, and Publishers (ASCAP), an organization that seeks royalty payments for public performances of music, is founded in New York City.

1914: **March** Comedian Charles Chaplin begins to develop the legendary character of the Little Tramp in the film *Mabel's Strange Predicament.*

1914: **November 3** The first American exhibition of African sculpture opens at the 291 Gallery in New York City.

1914: **December 3** The Isadorables, six European dancers trained by American dancer Isadora Duncan, perform at Carnegie Hall after escaping with her from war-torn Europe.

1915: Modern dancers Ruth St. Denis and Ted Shawn found the Denishawn School of Dancing in Los Angeles.

1915: **March 10** The Russian Symphony Orchestra plays the American debut performance of the symphony *Prometheus* by Aleksandr Scriabin at Carnegie Hall in New York City. Color images are projected onto a screen as part of the show.

1916: Newspaper publisher William Randolph Hearst inaugurates the *City Life* arts section as a supplement to his Sunday newspapers.

1916: **November** Inventor and radio pioneer Lee De Forest begins to transmit daily music broadcasts from his home in New York City.

1917: Showman George M. Cohan composes the song that was a musical call-to-arms during World War I: "Over There."

1917: Motion picture pioneer Cecil B. DeMille directs *The Little American,* a patriotic melodrama starring Mary Pickford.

1917: **October 27** Sixteen-year-old Russian-born violinist Jascha Heifetz makes his debut American performance at Carnegie Hall in New York City.

1918: The annual O. Henry Awards are inaugurated in honor of the short story writer O. Henry (pseudonym for William Sydney Porter).

1918: **December** The Theatre Guild is founded in New York City.

1919: *Maid of Harlem,* an all-black-cast musical starring "Fats" Waller, Mamie Smith, Johnny Dunn, and Perry Bradford, draws enthusiastic crowds at the Lincoln Theatre in New York City.

1919: **February 5** United Artists, an independent film distribution company, is founded by Charles Chaplin, Douglas Fairbanks, D. W. Griffith, and Mary Pickford.

Overview

During the twentieth century's second decade, the arts experienced what has come to be known as "The Little Renaissance," a rebirth in the style and content of the fine arts, literature, theater, and dance. American artists were moving away from established European traditions and developing new approaches to creating art. Many artists moved toward an abstract, not realistic, interpretation of subject matter. The content of artwork shifted, in part, from "higher level" subjects such as nature, religion, and portraits to more informal subjects. In fact, a group called the Ash Can school painted card players, boxing matches, and other subjects that previously had been considered unimportant or insignificant.

At the beginning of the decade, the blossoming film industry offered five- and ten-minute short movies shown in storefront theaters. By the end of the decade, longer feature-length films that used sophisticated techniques for telling stories were shown in larger theaters. The number of film production companies increased, and several major motion picture studios were established. No longer were the companies based almost solely on the East Coast. Instead the Los Angeles area, particularly Hollywood, was becoming attractive to film production units. Furthermore, audiences were curious about the actors who played in the "flickers" (as films were known), and eventually film producers identified the actors with on-screen credits. That procedure sparked the "star system," in which the most popular actors gained celebrity and wealth.

The theater, too, was in a state of change. The large theaters in New York City and other metropolitan areas were presenting elaborate variety shows with the latest songs and snappy skits by soon-to-be legendary performers Al Jolson, Fanny Brice, Will Rogers, and W. C. Fields. The music for these revues came, in great part, from the popular song-writing industry in New York City known as "Tin Pan Alley," where composers such as Irving Berlin, Walter Donaldson, W. C. Handy, and Albert and Harry Von Tilzer created popular tunes for sale in the form of sheet music. Serious plays by contemporary dramatists were being produced in "little theaters" that encouraged the creation of experimental theater. These plays emphasized the psychological state of the characters and analyzed the human condition.

Tastes in literature were changing as well, and writers increasingly explored American themes. A group of authors from the Midwest created interest in middle America as they began translating their small town and rural surroundings into powerful novels. Poetry flourished, as did many new, small magazines which published modern poetry for a growing readership.

The radio industry was in its infancy. Pioneers such as inventor Lee De Forest and future radio/television executive David Sarnoff were laying the framework for programming possibilities.

With the entrance of the United States into World War I, newspapers took on the responsibility of bringing war news to the public. Meanwhile, in Washington, D.C., representatives of the federal government established new media guidelines to apply to a nation at war.

Irving Berlin (1888–1989) Russian immigrant Irving Berlin rose from the poverty of New York City's lower east side tenements to become one of America's major composers. Between 1907 and 1966, he published 899 songs. Almost half became hits, and 282 became "top ten" numbers. They include "White Christmas," "Easter Parade," "There's No Business Like Show Business," "Always," and "God Bless America." Composer Jerome Kern said, "Irving Berlin has no place in American music. He *is* American music." *Photo reproduced courtesy of Library of Congress.*

Willa Cather (1873–1947) Willa Cather wrote fiction about America's agrarian (farming) past. Her style was a mix of nostalgia and realism. She spent her formative years in Nebraska, where her father farmed. Her first novel was *O Pioneers!* (1913), about Swedish immigrants on the Nebraska prairie. In 1918, she published her most famous novel, *My Antonia,* the tale of a Bohemian girl who endures tragedy and eventually finds spiritual revitalization. In 1922, Cather was awarded a Pulitzer Prize for *One of Ours,* a novel about a Midwestern hero in World War I. *Photo reproduced by permission of AP/Wide World Photos.*

Charles Chaplin (1889–1977) Charles Chaplin was the most famous silent film comedian. He is most famous for his character of the Little Tramp, a sometimes mischievous mustached man carrying a cane and wearing a derby, baggy trousers, and oversized shoes. In 1919, Chaplin became a founding partner in United Artists, an independent film distribution company. Among his most famous comedies are *The Immigrant* (1917), *Easy Street* (1917), *The Gold Rush* (1925), *City Lights* (1931), and *Modern Times* (1936). *Photo reproduced courtesy of Library of Congress.*

Robert Frost (1874–1963) The poems of Robert Frost capture the lifestyles, thoughts, and speech of the common New Englander. Frost, who eventually won four Pulitzer Prizes, worked on farms and also made his living as a mill worker and teacher. In his later years, he cultivated the image of the grandfatherly farmer-poet. One of America's most cherished memories of Frost in his elder years was his appearance at the inauguration of President John F. Kennedy (1917–1963) in 1961, when Frost recited his poem "The Gift Outright." *Photo reproduced courtesy of Library of Congress.*

D. W. Griffith (1875–1948) D. W. Griffith was the most significant motion picture director in the early days of cinema. While directing short films for the American Mutoscope and Biograph Company from 1908 to 1913, he developed techniques for making movies that have remained the conventional film language. His contributions include well-thought-out use of camera angles, close-ups and long-shots, and editing styles. Among the most well-known films that he produced, directed, and wrote are the epics *The Birth of a Nation* (1915) and *Intolerance* (1916). *Photo reproduced by permission of AP/Wide World Photos.*

W. C. Handy (1873–1958) W. C. Handy is known as "The Father of the Blues." The blues refers to songs of three-line verses featuring mournful lyrics and a melody that repeats flatted thirds and sevenths (blue notes). Handy did not invent this style of music; rather he adapted it from music being played by African American folk and spiritual singers. Throughout the first years of the twentieth century he composed works that helped to popularize the blues. In 1914, he wrote his legendary work, "The Saint Louis Blues." *Photo reproduced courtesy of Library of Congress.*

Mary Pickford (1893–1979) Her nickname was "America's Sweetheart" and, with a knowing smile and long blonde curls, Mary Pickford was the most beloved of the female stars of the silent screen. She starred in motion pictures from 1907 into the 1930s. She was also an astute businesswoman. In 1919, Pickford was one of the founding heads of United Artists and owner of The Mary Pickford Company. Her films include *Stella Maris* (1919), *Pollyanna* (1920), and *Little Lord Fauntleroy* (1921). *Photo reproduced courtesy of Library of Congress.*

John Reed (1887–1920) John Reed was a U.S. journalist and socialist political activist. In 1914, he made attempts to cover World War I in Russia. He found that his socialist viewpoint gave him access to the inner circle of the leaders of the Russian Revolution, who were trying to overthrow the brutal ruler Tsar Nicholas II (1868–1918) and establish a socialist state. In 1917, Reed was given a close view of the "October Revolution" when Vladimir Ilyich Lenin (1870–1924) and members of the "Workers and Peasants Government" entered Moscow and overthrew the provisional government. Reed's famed eyewitness account was published as *Ten Days That Shook the World* (1919). *Photo reproduced courtesy of Library of Congress.*

❖❖❖ **Topics in the News**

❖ AMERICAN ARTISTS REBEL

As the 1910s began, the National Academy of Design was the policy maker for fine art in the United States. The academy promoted and exhibited paintings representing only the genres of art that it deemed acceptable. These included the landscape paintings of Winslow Homer, the portraits of John Singer Sargent, and the impressionist works of William Merritt Chase. Impressionist works were so named because they recorded impressions of their subject matter without a great deal of detail. Excluded from the list were a number of painters who were working outside the academy's boundaries of acceptability. Among the "outcasts" were Robert Henri, John Sloan, William Glackens, George Luks, Everett Shinn, Ernest Lawson, Maurice Prendergast, and Arthur B.

Paintings like Pigeons *by John Sloan were part of a growing art movement known as the Ash Can school that focused on coarse, earthy subjects.*
Reproduced by permission of the Corbis Corporation.

Davies. These painters—who became known as The Eight—created art in a realistic style and, for the most part, concerned themselves with less refined, sometimes seedy aspects of urban life. In doing so, they were questioning the very definition of "art."

In 1908, The Eight arranged an exhibit of their works; all but two of the pieces on display, both by Henri, had been rejected by the academy. Then, in 1910, The Eight held a larger, open showing called the Exhibition of Independent Artists. Nearly two thousand people attended this exhibition, which was considered rebellious because it was not authorized by the academy. Further breaking with tradition, the Exhibition of Independent Artists established no juries (committees for judging) and awarded no prizes.

As the decade advanced, a growing number of artists joined the movement, including several whose coarse, earthy subjects secured them membership in what was known as the Ash Can school. The name stemmed from a painting by John Sloan (1871–1951) of a woman rummaging through a trash can. Among the most famous Ash Can paintings are Sloan's *McSorley's Bar* (1912) and *Cliff Dwellers* (1913), by George Bellows (1882–1925).

In addition to the Ash Can realists, painters such as Max Weber (1881–1961), Joseph Stella (1877–1946), and others joined the artists who had risen in rebellion against the academy and its rigid guidelines for art. Additionally, two photographers, Alfred Stieglitz (1864–1946) and Edward Steichen (1879–1973), helped to develop photography into a new kind of fine art. Later in the 1910s, American artists who had been influenced by other European abstract art movements became part of the ever-strengthening fellowship of modern artists.

❖ DANCERS BREAK THE RULES

In 1910, Russian dancer Anna Pavlova (1882–1931) first appeared on an American stage where she captivated audiences dancing the *Dying Swan* ballet. Her performance influenced mothers across the nation to dress their daughters in leotards and tutus and pay for ballet lessons. In 1916, Russian Sergey Diaghilev (1872–1929) brought the famed Ballet Russes to the United States, and Vaslav Nijinsky (1890–1950) made his American debut. The company offered a modern style of ballet that broke with the formal standards of classic choreography, incorporating dance steps with music and stage design. In addition, innovative modernist dancer Isadora Duncan (1878–1927) performed on stages in New York City and San Francisco in 1914 and 1917. These events forever changed American dance.

Even so, it was the dance team of New Jersey-born Ruth St. Denis (1878–1968) and Denver native Ted Shawn (1891–1972) that made the deepest impression with the American public. St. Denis had been a dancer in vaudeville and in Broadway revues until she teamed with Shawn, a former theology student. The couple, who met in 1914 and married in 1915, believed that spirituality could be expressed through body movement. Their dances emphasized the connection of mind, body, and soul. In 1915, they established Denishawn, a dance company and school, in Los Angeles. During the next seventeen years, Denishawn dancers, including their star pupil Martha Graham (1894–1991), performed original choreography across the nation. Several of their dances were purely American with subjects such as cowboys or industrial workers, while other were influenced by Orientalism, an involvement with Asian culture that was fashionable in the United States and Europe at the time.

❖ LITERATURE: AN AMERICAN VOICE EMERGES

A number of significant American novels in the 1910s were penned by writers from the Midwest, including Nebraskan Willa Cather (1873–1947); Booth Tarkington (1869–1946) and Theodore Dreiser (1871–1945), both from Indiana; Edgar Lee Masters (1869–1950) and Carl Sandburg (1878–1967) of Illinois; Ohioan Sherwood Anderson (1876–1941); and

Ruth St. Denis and her husband Ted Shawn made a deep impression on the American dance scene. Reproduced by permission of Archive Photos, Inc.

Hamlin Garland (1860–1940) who grew up in Minnesota, Iowa, and South Dakota. So strong was the Midwestern influence that Chicago became the center of a literary Renaissance during the 1910s.

These authors' writings emphasized realism and highlighted topics related to the American experience. The European influence of earlier decades was fading, and literature such as Tarkington's *Penrod* (1914), Anderson's *Winesburg, Ohio* (1919), and Cather's prairie novels *O Pioneers!* (1913), *The Song of the Lark* (1915), and *My Antonia* (1918) told stories in which the regional American settings were as powerful an element as the characters themselves. The urban immigrant experience was chronicled in such novels as *The Rise of David Levinsky* (1917), the fictional biography of a Jewish businessman, by Abraham Cahan (1860–1951).

Established novelists Edith Wharton (1862–1937) and Henry James (1843–1916) continued writing during the decade; however, their influence on other American writers was limited by the fact that both were living in Europe by the early 1910s. Wharton's writing often was gender-oriented, in that she emphasized society's treatment of women. Several of her novels concentrated on life in Europe, while her novel *Ethan Frome* (1911) was set in the rural Berkshires of Massachusetts. James, who became a British citizen in 1915, often wrote about Americans traveling in Europe.

Poetry also was a popular form of literature, and a growing number of new poets published in magazines such as *Smart Set*, *The Atlantic Monthly*,

The Armory Show and Its Legacy

On February 17, 1913, an enormous exhibition of new-style art opened at the Sixty-Ninth Regiment Armory on Lexington Avenue in New York City. It was organized by a number of independent artists who had formed the Association of American Painters and Sculptors in 1911. Seventy-five thousand viewers attended the show, which included new and established European and American artists. The list of participants is impressive. Included were:

Established Europeans	**European Newcomers**	**Established Americans**
Paul Cezanne	Constantin Brancusi	Mary Cassatt
Vincent van Gogh	Marcel Duchamp	Childe Hassam
Paul Gauguin	Henri Matisse	James McNeill Whistler
Edouard Manet	Francis Picabia	Albert Pinkham Ryder
Claude Monet	Pablo Picasso	**American Newcomers**
Camille Pissarro	Odilon Redon	George Bellows
Pierre Auguste Renoir		Marsden Hartley
Auguste Rodin		Edward Hopper
Georges Seurat		John Marin
Henri de Toulouse-Lautrec		Joseph Stella

and *Vanity Fair.* To further accommodate the market for modern poetry, a number of small-press magazines were founded, such as *Poetry* (Chicago, 1912), in which T. S. Eliot (1888–1965) published his famous "The Love Song of J. Alfred Prufrock" (1915); *The Poetry Journal* (Boston, 1912); *The Glebe* (Ridgefield, NJ; 1913); and *Others* (Grantwood, NJ; 1915).

The formats of new poetry offered an escape from older verse, taking on increasingly abstract styles. Gertrude Stein (1874–1946) used words in an innovative manner, stressing that poetry should be read aloud. She and Vachel Lindsay (1879–1931) were among the first American poets to give public readings of their work. Ezra Pound (1885–1972), with Hilda Doolittle (also known as H. D. Doolittle) (1886–1961) and Richard Aldington (1892–1962), created Imagism, a literary concept that avoided unneeded words, called for direct treatment of the subject, and favored musical phrasing over strict meter (the orderly arrangement of words in a poem). By mid-decade, a number of important American poets had relocated to Paris or London.

Mary Pickford and Douglas Fairbanks in a scene from the film version of Taming of the Shrew. *Pickford and Fairbanks are just two of the first movie stars.*
Reproduced by permission of AP/Wide World Photos.

❖ MOVIES: THE BUSINESS, THE STUDIOS, THE STARS, AND THE PICTURES

By 1910, the motion picture business had been in existence for more than a decade. Inventor Thomas Edison (1847–1931) controlled patents on many inventions that made movie-making possible. Although Edison

The Birth of a Nation Makes
History Come to Life while Making History

D. W. Griffith could not have realized the enduring significance of his historical film epic *The Birth of a Nation* (1915) when it was in production. The film is a spellbinding melodrama of two families who wind up on opposing sides during the American Civil War. It offers exciting battle sequences, reproductions of historic events, and a captivating story of people who suffered from the war. Unfortunately, it also features one of the most bigoted depictions of African Americans in the history of the cinema. In its climax, the sympathetic Southern white characters are saved by the Ku Klux Klan (KKK). Although this real-life racist group had disbanded in 1869, the excitement of this blockbuster motion picture led to the rebirth of the KKK in late 1915.

and others experimented with synchronized sound, the movies remained silent until the end of the 1920s, when the problems of synchronizing sound with the picture and amplifying sound were solved.

Movie-making was an East Coast-based industry during its first years, and most of the films were produced in the New York City and New Jersey area. In 1908, The Motion Picture Patents Company (MPPC) was formed by the nine leading film companies (Edison, Biograph, Vitagraph, Essanay, Lubin, Selig, Kalem, Melies, and Pathe), along with inventor George Armat and distributor George Kleine. The organization was a trust (a combination of companies working together to reduce competition) that intended to put out of business any film companies that did not join their group. Even as the decade began, a number of film companies were moving their production facilities to other locations, including southern Florida and California. One of the reasons for the move was the attraction of good weather and lots of sunshine. Another was to avoid dealing with the MPPC. In 1917, the MPPC was disbanded by U.S. law as an illegal trust.

The length of motion pictures changed as the decade advanced. In 1910, movies lasted between five minutes (a split-reeler) and eleven minutes (a one-reeler). In December 1910, director D.W. Griffith (1875–1948) made *His Trust/His Trust Fulfilled,* a two-reel film, for the American Mutoscope and Biograph Company. He wanted it to be seen in one sitting, but his bosses released it in two parts. Audiences craved uninterrupted storytelling and eventually, in 1911, two-reel films began to be exhibited. One of the first was Griffith's film adaptation of the celebrated poem *Enoch Arden,* by Alfred Lord Tennyson (1809–1892).

By 1911, the film industry in Italy was making motion pictures that lasted more than one hour. When these were shown in the United States in 1911 and 1912, their popularity sparked the production of feature-length American-made movies. Two of the most significant films of the decade were the controversial Civil War epic *The Birth of a Nation* (1915) and the cinema masterpiece *Intolerance* (1916), which intertwined four stories. Each was produced, directed, and scripted by Griffith, and each was three hours long.

Another film maker whose movies stand out in a decade filled with innovative movie makers is Cecil B. DeMille (1881–1959). In 1914, DeMille directed *The Squaw Man,* the first feature-length Western shot in Hollywood. Later he made films that were enjoyed by audiences who were experiencing a loosening of traditional Victorian morality in the post-World War I "Jazz Age" at the end of the decade.

Slapstick comedies were popular with American audiences. Producer Mack Sennett (1880–1960) was known as "the king of comedy." In 1912, he set up his own independent production company, Keystone. This studio was a comedy factory, turning out several short films per week, many of which featured a dimwitted police force called The Keystone Kops. Each short featured a simple plot that was peppered with a string of comic gags. Most of the gags were highly physical, and featured chase sequences. In December 1913, Sennett hired a British music hall performer and mime named Charles Chaplin (1889–1977). Soon Chaplin would become the most famous comedian in motion pictures.

In 1910, audiences went to see movies without regard for titles, production companies, directors, or actors. By mid-decade however, the star system was developing at a rapid pace. In the early years of the decade, audiences could only hope to see their favorite actors by chance because the film producers did not promote individual performers. There were ripples of discontent among moviegoers; they were unhappy about the anonymity of movie actors and wanted the studios to identify and advertise featured performers. The studio heads refused to divulge names, fearing that the popular performers would ask for higher salaries. In 1912, the bosses gave in when they realized that ticket sales rose when the actors were recognized by audiences. The first stars of the cinema were identified with the studios for which they worked. Florence Lawrence (1886–1938) was "the Biograph Girl," and Florence Turner (1885–1946) "the Vitagraph Girl." That approach was dropped after Mary Pickford (1893–1979), who moved from one studio to another, remained a favorite with fans. Other early screen stars included Lillian Gish, Douglas Fairbanks, Gloria Swanson, Mabel Normand, Blanche

Sweet, Maurice Costello, Francis X. Bushman, Clara Kimball Young, and western standouts Tom Mix and William S. Hart.

❖ MUSIC: UPTOWN AND DOWNTOWN

The public's interest in symphonic music (music played by large orchestras) grew as the music became more available through the production and sale of 78 revolutions-per-minute (rpm) recordings, radio broadcasts, and the spread of symphonic orchestras in cities across the nation. In the midst of the general appeal for this type of music among Americans, most of the music being played in concert settings was the product of European composers and was often performed by European musicians. Further, if an American wanted to train to become a composer or musician, he or she was expected to study abroad in a major European conservatory of music.

Ironically, as Americans appreciated listening to the works of such new European composers as Igor Stravinsky (1882–1971) and Sergey Prokofiev (1891–1953), an unrecognized American composer named Charles Ives (1874–1954) was writing works that would later be considered his finest, most enduring creations. Even so, he would not be acclaimed as a great American symphonic composer for several more decades. The Connecticut-based composer drew upon older formats of classical music but also used bold, experimental touches in his works. For instance, he repeated certain themes several times simultaneously in different keys or time signatures. In 1915, Ives wrote the piece that remains his most popular: *Second Sonata for Piano, Concord, Mass., 1840–1869*. It features movements titled "Emerson," "Hawthorne," "The Alcotts," and "Thoreau," all named after famous American writers. The fact that his work was then unfairly overlooked by the classical music community is best demonstrated by his winning of the Pulitzer Prize for music in 1947 for his *Third Symphony*, a work that was written in 1911, but performed for the first time in 1945.

With opera, the emphasis also was on the European composers. Among the most popular new operas staged during the 1910s in American cities were *Der Rosenkavalier* (1911) and *Ariadne auf Naxos* (1912), by German composer Richard Strauss (1864–1949). Still, Americans were encouraged to pursue this musical genre. In fact, during the 1910s, the New York Metropolitan Opera House (the Met), the foremost opera company in America, set up an annual competition, with a $10,000 prize, for the best new American opera. The first winner was Horatio Parker (1863–1919) of Yale University for *Mona,* which premiered at the Met on March 14, 1912.

Meanwhile, popular music for the masses was being produced in the form of sheet music, sold in most five-and-dime stores across the country.

This music could be played in the home, and it cost a penny to ten cents per song sheet. With the rapid rise of radio programming and the recording industry during the decade, the mass marketing of popular songs increased. The production and distribution of popular songs stemmed from what had come to be known as "Tin Pan Alley." Based in New York City, this small but prolific songwriting industry actually had been concentrated in an alley on West Twenty-Eighth Street between Broadway and Sixth Avenue at the end of the nineteenth century. By 1910, the many offices of Tin Pan Alley songwriters, producers, and marketers had spread to other nearby neighborhoods.

The leading composers of popular tunes during the decade included George M. Cohan, brothers Albert and Harry Von Tilzer, Harry Ruby, Gus Kahn, Sam M. Lewis, Walter Donaldson, Joe Young, and Richard Whiting. Most successful of all was Irving Berlin (1888–1989), who composed more than three hundred songs during the decade and formed his own music company. Various categories of popular songs included ethnic novelty songs, comedy numbers, "home songs" (which were sweet tunes for women to play on their parlor pianos), "coon songs" (which emphasized aspects of African American lifestyles), and romantic ballads.

The African American influence on Tin Pan Alley music was strong. Syncopated, ragtime rhythms that had been part of African American jazz music in the first few years of the century now were entering into popular tunes. Berlin's "Alexander's Ragtime Band"(1911)—inspired by ragtime music but lacking a feature called syncopation, in which a weak beat is stressed—was one of the most popular songs of its time. Almost singlehandedly, it sparked a ragtime fashion in popular music. A string of black composers, including Scott Joplin, James Scott, Eubie Blake, and Shelton Brooks, wrote hit songs. Joplin (1868–1917) published his second complete ragtime opera, *Treemonisha,* in 1911. His first one, *A Guest of Honor,* had appeared in 1903. W.C. Handy (1873–1958), whose "The Memphis Blues" was published in two versions in 1910 and 1912, was a pioneer in popularizing the form of jazz called the blues, a type of music that dates from the days of slavery, when African American slaves sang spirituals and work chants in the field.

❖ POPULAR THEATER AND RISING THEATER MOVEMENTS

Throughout the 1910s, the most popular forms of theater included music. These appealing productions were either called musicals, which were thinly plotted stories with song numbers to break up the action, or musical revues, which were separate musical numbers held together by a common theme and ending with an elaborate production number. In future decades, these forms of musical theater would take on a more formal structure and become shows that dramatically integrated musical numbers into a plot. The first musical theater to effectively do so was *Show Boat* in 1927.

The most memorable musical revues were produced by Florenz Ziegfeld (1867–1932). His annual *Follies* ran from 1907 to 1931. The shows, which featured stylish sets, new musical compositions by top Tin Pan Alley and other contemporary composers, comic sketches, and a line-up of beautiful Ziegfeld Girls, opened in New York City and then toured cities across the country. Among the stars of the Ziegfeld *Follies* were musical artists and comedians W. C. Fields, Will Rogers, Fanny Brice, Eddie Cantor, Irene Castle, and Billie Burke. Recognizing the immense popularity of the *Follies,* the Shubert Brothers (Sam S., Jacob J., and Lee) produced their own version of the annual revue, titled the *Passing Show,* which began in 1912 and also became very fashionable.

To accommodate the enthusiasm for musical revues, the Shuberts opened the sixteen-hundred-seat Winter Garden theater on Broadway between Fiftieth and Fifty-First Streets on March 20, 1911. The first show was *La Belle Paree,* a musical revue featuring Broadway newcomer Al Jolson (1886–1950). Jolson would be the headliner at the Winter Garden for the next fifteen years. He was a precursor to the modern-day superstar.

Florenz Ziegfeld produced the most memorable musical revues. His annual Follies *ran from 1907 to 1931. Reproduced by permission of Archive Photos, Inc.*

Dramas also were a popular form of theater. The most traditional dramas spoke of the way life ought to be, and featured happy endings. During the decade, however, more plays were produced that focused on how life actually *was.* These new plays explored the psychological state of the characters. A pioneer in this movement was Eugene O'Neill (1888–1953). During the 1910s, O'Neill was still in the early stages of his play writing, which truly blossomed during the next decade. In the 1910s, he and other serious-minded dramatists were involved in a new manner of stage production called The Little Theater Movement, in which short plays and experimental theater were produced by companies that resided separately from larger, mainstream theaters. The Henry Street Settlement in Lower Manhattan and the Provincetown Players, which had theaters on the far tip of Cape Cod, Massachusetts, and in Greenwich Village, New

York, are examples of small theater groups that influenced the mainstream theater of the 1920s by presenting experimental works during the 1910s.

As is true of each twentieth century decade, the theater of the 1910s featured actors who were more popular than the works in which they appeared. The Barrymore family, particularly siblings Ethel (1879–1959), Lionel (1878–1954), and John (1882–1942), delighted audiences in stage dramas throughout the decade. Among their hit plays were: *Mid-Channel* (1910), by Arthur Wing Pinero (1855–1934), with Ethel; *Justice* (1916), by John Galsworthy (1867–1933), with John; and *The Copperhead* (1918), by Augustus Thomas (1857–1934), with Lionel. Another star of dramatic theater was Laurette Taylor (1884–1946), whose appearance in *Peg o' My Heart* (1912) scored a hit with audiences.

❖ NEWSPAPERS COVER WORLD WAR I FROM DIFFERENT PERSPECTIVES

Writing the news of the day might seem to be a straightforward business, but newspapers reported regional and world events with a remarkable number of biases during the 1910s. Corruption among newspaper publishing companies was widespread during the first decade of the century. In 1911, Will Irwin (1873–1948), a former reporter for the *New York Sun* and editor of *McClure's* magazine, published an in-depth research study called "The American Newspaper" in *Collier's*, a popular magazine. In it, he demonstrated that certain newspapers printed the news with honesty and integrity, while others tailored the news to the advantage of their owners and advertisers.

Powerful newspaper publisher William Randolph Hearst used his papers to editorialize that the United States should remain out of World War I. Reproduced courtesy of Library of Congress.

Taking an antiwar stance was not uncommon among the African American press and various papers representing immigrant groups after World War I started in 1914. If the war was not going to further the progress of a particular segment in American society, then there was no use favoring the fighting. That remained the case until some of these antiwar presses were criticized for publishing antipatriotic statements. The passing of the 1917 Espionage Act and the 1918 Sedition Act, which were passed after the United States entered the war in 1917, allowed government officials to suppress newspapers that did not submit to official U.S.

William Randolph Hearst Takes an Unpopular Stand on World War I

. . . .

William Randolph Hearst (1863–1951) was one of the most powerful newspaper publishers in the country at the start of World War I, and during the war he became one of America's most hated citizens. His newspaper chain included the *New York American,* the *San Francisco Examiner,* and several other papers.

From the start of the war in Europe in 1914, Hearst's papers editorialized that America should remain out of the war. Even when America entered the conflict after three years of neutrality, Hearst maintained his controversial stance despite the strong criticism of much of his readership and other newspapers.

policies concerning the war. During 1917 and 1918, many socialist and foreign language papers were targeted. Some closed, while others relented and switched their editorials to reflect prowar policies.

In 1917, President Woodrow Wilson (1856–1924) signed into existence the Committee on Public Information (CPI) to assure the promotion of an official government war policy and give the American public "the feeling of partisanship that comes with full, frank statements concerning the conduct of the public business." Newspaperman George Creel (1876–1953) was named chairman of the CPI. To some, Creel and his committee of expert advisers and journalists sought to supply the public with a federal war policy. To others, it seemed that the committee was waging a propaganda campaign to encourage all Americans to believe in the same policies as the government. Particularly emphasized in the Creel committee's "information" was a ferocious hatred for Germans, who often were referred to as "the Huns." The policies expounded by the CPI found their way into the newspapers, magazines, and even the novels and movies of the day.

❖ RADIO IN ITS INFANCY

From 1906 to 1919, a young Russian immigrant named David Sarnoff (1891–1971) worked for the American branch of the Marconi Wireless Company. He was one of the company's most capable telegraph operators. In 1916, Sarnoff proposed a "Radio Music Box" to his superiors, but his memorandum either was rejected or went unread. The radio industry soon would become the nation's in-home source for information and entertainment. Sarnoff would be one of the key players in designing and heading the new industry. During World War I, the Marconi Company became government controlled. After the war, it was reorganized as the Radio Corporation of America (RCA), and Sarnoff became its commercial manager. Thirteen years later, he was named president of RCA, which eventually grew into a media giant whose power and influence transcended his own proposed "Radio Music Box."

For More Information

BOOKS

Adair, Gene. *Thomas Alva Edison: Inventing the Electric Age.* New York: Oxford University Press, 1996.

Applebaum, Stanley, editor. *The New York Stage: Famous Productions in Photographs.* New York: Dover Publications, 1976.

Beardsley, John. *Henry James.* Broomall, PA: *Chelsea House,* 2001.

Beardsley, John. *Pablo Picasso.* New York: Harry N. Abrams, 1991.

Bloom, Harold, ed. *Edith Wharton.* Philadelphia: Chelsea House, 2001.

Blum, Daniel. *Great Stars of the American Stage.* New York: Grosset & Dunlap, 1952.

Blum, Daniel, enlarged by John Willis. *A Pictorial History of the American Theatre.,* 6th ed. New York: Crown Publishers, 1986.

Blum, Daniel. *A Pictorial History of the Silent Screen.* New York: Putnam, 1953.

Bober, Natalie S. *A Restless Spirit: The Story of Robert Frost.* New York: Henry Holt, 1991.

Cohen, Daniel. *Yellow Journalism: Scandal, Sensationalism and Gossip in the Media.* Brookfield, CT: Twenty-First Century Books, 2000.

Ellis, Rex. *With a Banjo on My Knee: A Musical Journey from Slavery to Freedom.* New York: Franklin Watts, 2001.

Gottfried, Ted. *The American Media.* New York: Franklin Watts, 1997.

Halliwell, Sarah, ed. *The Twentieth Century: Pre-1945 Artists, Writers, and Composers.* Austin, TX: Raintree Steck-Vaughn, 1998.

Hanson, Patricia King, executive ed. *The American Film Institute Catalog of Motion Pictures Produced in the United States, Feature Films, 1911–1920.* Berkeley, Los Angeles, London: University of California Press, 1988.

Janson, H. W., and Anthony F. Janson. *History of Art for Young People,* 5th edition. New York: Harry Abrams, 1997.

Katz, Ephraim. *The Film Encyclopedia,* 4th edition. New York: HarperResource, 2001.

Leach, William. *Edith Wharton.* New York: Chelsea House, 1987.

Maltin, Leonard, ed. *Leonard Maltin's Movie Encyclopedia.* New York: Dutton, 1994.

O'Brien, Sharon, and Martin Duberman. *Willa Cather.* New York: Chelsea House, 1995.

Orgill, Roxane. *Shout, Sister, Shout! Ten Girl Singers Who Shaped a Century.* New York: Margaret McElderry, 2001.

Schroeder, Alan. *Charles Chaplin: The Beauty of Silence.* New York, Franklin Watts, 1997.

Slide, Anthony. *Early American Cinema.* New York: A.S. Barnes, 1970.

Vaughan, William H. T. *Encyclopedia of Artists.* New York: Oxford University Press, 2000.

WEB SITES

American Cultural History: The Twentieth Century, 1910–1919. http://www.nhmccd. cc.tx.us/contracts/lrc/kc/decade10.html (accessed on August 2, 2002).

American Masters-D.W. Griffith. http://www.pbs.org/wnet/americanmasters/database/ griffith_d.html (accessed on August 2, 2002).

Irving Berlin: In and Out of Time. http://www.kcmetro.cc.mo.us/pennvalley/biology/ lewis/crosby/berlin.htm (accessed on August 2, 2002).

Business and the Economy

1910: Nearly one-third of America's coal miners belong to labor unions, compared to 10 percent of the labor force in other industries.

1910: *Life* magazine observes that banker and financier J. P. Morgan is so powerful that he should be crowned monarch of the United States and purchase Europe.

1910: June 18 Congress enacts the Mann-Elkins Act to enlarge the powers of the Interstate Commerce Commission, allowing it to regulate cable, wireless, telephone, and telegraph companies.

1911: May 15 The Supreme Court rules that Standard Oil Company of New Jersey must be dissolved as an unreasonable combination in restraint of trade under antitrust laws.

1911: May 29 The Supreme Court declares that the American Tobacco Company is an illegal combination in restraint of trade and must dissolve under antitrust laws.

1912: Radical labor leader Elizabeth Gurley Flynn and birth control advocate Margaret Sanger help to organize a strike of 20,000 textile workers in Lawrence, Massachusetts. After beat-ings and police attacks, the returning workers are given better wages.

1912: May 1 Ship safety regulations are issued by federal inspectors following the sinking of the *Titanic*. Steamships must carry an appropriate number of lifeboats to accommodate all the passengers.

1913: The 792-foot high Woolworth Building opens in New York City, symbolizing the wealth of a growing national commercial economy.

1913: Grand Central Terminal opens in New York City.

1913: The completion of the Panama Canal marks an opportunity for new trade possibilities between Atlantic and Pacific nations.

1913: December 23 The Federal Reserve System is established by the Federal Reserve Act, and the nation is divided into twelve districts with a Federal Reserve Bank in each. A board of seven men controls the system, which all national banks must join. The system is meant to provide stable banking policies for the nation.

1914: January 10 President Woodrow Wilson calls for the strengthening of the country's antitrust laws.

1914: **September 26** The Federal Trade Commission Act is adopted to stop unfair competition in interstate trade.

1915: **January 15** The first transcontinental telephone line becomes available for service between New York City and San Francisco.

1915: **October 15** Private American banks extend a loan of $500 million to France and Great Britain, which are involved in fighting Germany in World War I.

1915: **December 10** The one-millionth Model T automobile rolls off the assembly line at the Ford Motor Company's Highland Park, Michigan, plant.

1916: Boeing Aircraft designs and produces its first model, a biplane.

1916: **July 17** The Federal Farm Loan Act passes in Congress, setting up twelve Farm Loan Banks to extend long-term loans to farmers.

1917: **April 6** The United States enters World War I.

1917: **April 24** The Liberty Loan Act is adopted to allow the public sale of bonds and the extension of loans to Allied powers fighting in World War I.

1917: **December 18** Congress proposes to adopt the Eighteenth Amendment, prohibiting the manufacture, sale, or transportation of "intoxicating liquors."

1917: **December 26** The U.S. Railroad Administration takes over the country's railroads to aid transportation of war-related goods. They remain under government control until 1920.

1918: **March 21** The Railroad Control Act authorizes the government to operate railroads on a regional basis and pay railroad companies while the lines remain under federal control.

1918: **April 8** The National War Labor Board is set up to settle labor disputes in order to avoid disrupting war production.

1918: **July 16** The federal government takes charge of the nation's telephone and telegraph systems.

1919: **January 29** The Eighteenth Amendment, which prohibited the transportation and sale of alcoholic beverages, is ratified by Congress.

1919: **September 9** The Boston police force goes on strike, leaving citizens without protection.

Overview

The United States entered the 1910s as a country with a relatively undeveloped economy that operated in isolation from foreign interests. The inauguration of Woodrow Wilson as U.S. president in 1913, and with innovations from an up-and-coming new breed of bankers and businessmen, this ten-year-period would bring awesome changes to the U.S. economy. Particularly with its entry into World War I (1914–18), the United States proved to the nations of the world that it had become a modern industrial power. Because the growth of the economy resulted in jarring changes to the structure of business and the labor force, government legislation and labor reforms were sought to safeguard the lifestyles of middle-class and working-class Americans.

At the start of the decade, many American workers remained on farms or were employed in small stores, factories, or mills. As the decade advanced, workers moved into big cities to take higher paying jobs in large industrial plants. With the rise of modern factory and assembly line techniques, jobs became more dependent upon machinery and many in the work force became drudges in monotonous, unskilled labor. The American labor force became dehumanized as modern technology experts analyzed the science of worker efficiency. The difficulty of the workers' condition within the modern factory system and the desire for better wages and improved work conditions led to a significant rise in membership in labor unions and an increase in strikes and other labor actions. Immigrant workers struggled for rights as they sought to build quality lifestyles for themselves and their families. Women, too, were becoming more aware of their rights in the workplace.

One reason for the increase in manufacturing jobs was the public's expanded taste for consumer goods. What had once been a conservative-spending public that relied on farming, general stores, and small groceries for food and goods was becoming a nation of enthusiastic consumers. Shopping once had been a necessary part of the weekly routine; now it was becoming a form of recreation. Retailers (those who sell products directly to the public) developed modern techniques for displaying and selling goods, and the advertising industry grew alongside the huge retail business.

President Wilson set about to enact a reform program called "The New Freedom." He hoped to open the U.S. economy to global interests and eliminate corporate trusts (combinations of companies run by a powerful few that discouraged competition in the marketplace). Wilson's administration intended to use the power of the federal government to ensure the American people that the American way of life would continue in the face of so many changes brought about by modern big business. Rather than alienating the heads of modern corporations, Wilson asked for their advice in drawing up legislation. By doing so, he had to make many compromises in writing laws, but he gained the cooperation of the biggest economic powers in the nation. This new relationship between government and big business proved to be a blueprint for twentieth-century U.S. economics.

The enactment of new tariff legislation (laws regarding the taxes placed on imported or exported goods), banking reforms, and an income tax were a few of the ways that the administration furthered the development of the United States as an economic power while protecting the American ideal of democracy.

Bernard M. Baruch (1870–1965) Bernard M. Baruch began his financial career as a Wall Street stock market speculator whose risky investments proved very profitable. Always a student of business methods, in later years he often gave advice about global trade issues to U.S. presidents. In 1918, Woodrow Wilson named him chairman of the War Industries Board, and he advised Franklin Roosevelt during World War II (1939–45). During the administration of Harry Truman, Baruch was the American delegate to the United Nations Atomic Energy Commission where he proposed the "Baruch Plan" for regulating atomic energy worldwide. *Photo courtesy of the Library of Congress.*

Howard E. Coffin (1873–1937) Howard E. Coffin was the most prominent member of an elite group of American engineers who advocated industrial readiness for the country's entrance into World War I. His work for the U.S. government's Naval Consulting Board in 1915 laid the foundations for the later activities of the War Industries Board, which mobilized American industries to produce the supplies needed for war. Coffin emphasized the importance of standardization in the manufacturing industry, the creation of an inventory of natural resources, and the coordinated efforts of labor and business with the government.

William "Billy" C. Durant (1861–1947) William "Billy" C. Durant was a dreamer and empire builder whose focus was on the automobile industry. On September 16, 1908, Durant incorporated an entity that he called General Motors with only two thousand dollars in capital. He acquired the Buick, Oldsmobile, Cadillac, and Oakland (later Pontiac) companies under the new corporate name. During the 1910s, he bought five more automobile companies, including Chevrolet, for which he personally oversaw the design and building of the early models. He was fired from General Motors in 1920 and had to declare bankruptcy in 1936. *Photo courtesy of the Library of Congress.*

Frank B. Gilbreth (1868–1924) Engineer Frank B. Gilbreth and his wife Lillian Moller Gilbreth, also an engineer, pioneered concepts of measuring the efficiency of factory work that Lillian termed "The Quest for the One Best Way." Through time and motion studies, using a motion picture camera, the Gilbreths eliminated wasted movements from factory work. Frank began as a disciple of Philadelphia engineer Frederick W. Taylor (1856–1915), whose concept of "Taylorism" restructured the factory by measuring and extracting the maximum output for each worker. The

Gilbreths later developed their own systems. Their studies of fatigue's impact on the mind and their motion study of sixteen hand movements called "Therbligs" contributed to the couple's larger concept of living all aspects of life in an efficient manner. *Photo reproduced by permission of the Corbis Corporation.*

Samuel Gompers (1850–1924) London-born Samuel Gompers was the most influential labor leader in American history before the epic strikes of the 1930s. As president of the American Federation of Labor (AFL) from 1886 to 1924, he opposed militant political unionism and during the 1910s took a moderate course in developing relations between labor and the government. By doing so, Gompers helped trade unions gain the respect of the federal government and the general public. During his four-decade tenure, he became increasingly exclusive in his ideas about union membership, shunning immigrants, women, socialists, and unskilled laborers in favor of skilled male workers. *Photo courtesy of the Library of Congress.*

John Mitchell (1870–1919) John Mitchell was a forceful labor leader who worked to improve the working conditions of miners in the United States. A miner himself from the age of twelve, Mitchell understood the needs of this workforce and, as a labor leader, he won the miners higher wages, shorter workdays, and the right to form grievance committees. As president of the United Mine Workers of America (1899–1908) and vice president of the American Federation of Labor (1899–1914), Mitchell leaned towards conservatism and advocated cooperative relations between labor and big business, a stance that angered some labor factions. *Photo reproduced by permission of Archive Photos, Inc.*

Edward Alsworth Ross (1866–1951) Standing six feet, six inches in height, Edward Alsworth Ross was an impressive speaker on behalf of the Progressive movement, whose supporters worked to create economic, political, and social reform in the United States through increased government regulation. Author of *Sin and Society* (1907), an influential treatise on Progressivism, Ross taught at the University of Wisconsin, Madison, from 1906 to 1937. He lectured across the country, criticizing the modern industrial system and expressing sympathy for the social conditions under which factory workers lived. A pioneer in economics, sociology, and social reform, Ross believed that democracy should elevate the average person above inherited social status. *Photo reproduced courtesy of Library of Congress.*

◆◆◆ *Topics in the News* . . . .

❖ **ECONOMIC FOUNDATIONS OF
TWENTIETH-CENTURY AMERICA**

In the early years of the decade, most Americans lived in rural areas, where farming and self-employment in small businesses were common means of support. The world of big business—railroads, banks, insurance companies, steel, meatpacking, and oil refining—was controlled by trusts (combinations of companies run by a powerful few that discouraged competition in the marketplace). At this time, the government did not play a large role in American business policies, and the nation remained relatively isolated from international trade. But World War I (1914–18), fought in Europe and known at the time as "The Great War," marked a new era in international relations and business.

In July 1914, Austria declared war on Serbia. In August, Germany declared war on Russia and France and invaded Belgium. The same month, Great Britain declared war on Germany. The United States decided to remain neutral—that is, it declared that it wouldn't take sides—in the conflict. By the end of that year, Great Britain had been attacked by Germany, and within the coming year, virtually all of Europe was engulfed in "The Great War." The "Triple Entente," later known as the Allied Powers, or simply the Allies (Great Britain, France, and Russia), fought against the Central Powers (originally known as the "Triple Alliance" of Germany, Austria-Hungary, and Italy; Italy would drop out of the alliance, and was replaced by Turkey and Bulgaria). Despite the American desire to remain uninvolved, the country officially entered the fighting in 1917 due to Germany's use of unrestricted submarine warfare. The United States sided with the Allied Powers and had become the main source of supplies for the nations fighting against the Central Powers, as well as the world's largest creditor (lender of money to governments and businesses).

Woodrow Wilson (1856–1924) was a Democrat who became the twenty-eighth president of the United States in 1913. He had campaigned as an opponent of big business. He and other politicians with similar philosophies appealed to many Americans who saw the greedy powers of big business as threats to the American economy and the American way of life that valued initiative and determination on the part of the individual, and the opportunity to work in an atmosphere of fair competition.

Wilson's reform program was called the "New Freedom." With this program, he hoped to eliminate the corporate trusts, open the economic market to international trade through reforms on tariffs (taxes paid on imports and exports), and use the power of the federal government to pro-

 One of the most ambitious and controversial concepts to come from Woodrow Wilson's administration was the War Industries Board (WIB), created in July 1917. Originally, it was a subordinate body to the Council of National Defense, but in March 1918, the WIB became a separate agency with Wall Street financier Bernard M. Baruch (1870–1965) as its head. The purpose of the WIB was to mobilize the nation's resources for war, while protecting the economy's basic structure and character for the upcoming peace. For example, the agency implemented modern business methods to streamline the production of war materials. The agency vanished as soon as the war ended. Its most lasting legacy is that it brought industry into close and regular interaction with congressional committees, cabinet departments, and executive agencies.

tect the American people from price gouging and unfair labor practices of big business. During his eight years in the White House, Wilson enacted policies and legislation to strengthen America's position in the world market and make big business more mindful of American ideals.

As early as 1913, the Wilson administration backed the Underwood-Simmons Tariff Act to promote free trade on an international basis. Until its passing, the United States placed a 40 percent tax on imports (goods produced in other countries). This made the purchase of lower-priced foreign goods impractical and difficult for average Americans. The act lowered tariffs on incoming goods to an average of 29 percent. In 1914, the Clayton Antitrust Act was passed as a supplement to the Sherman Antitrust Act of 1890, which had been passed to keep large companies in any particular business or industry from banding together and controlling the market, forcing up prices. The Clayton Antitrust Act outlawed monopolies (companies that had complete ownership of a product or service, and thereby controlled supply and price of that product or service). Also, the act legalized peaceful strikes, picketing, and organized boycotting (publicly refusing, as a group, to buy from a company as a means of showing disapproval of its practices, and encouraging the public to do so as well) on the part of the unions. Next, Wilson's administration set up the Federal Trade Commission as an investigative body to help prevent unfair business practices and to maintain fair competition in the marketplace.

This program, which was supported by those in favor of the Progressive movement, threatened the interests of a handful of economically powerful men such as John D. Rockefeller (1839–1937), who had ruthlessly gained control of the oil industry in the form of Standard Oil Trust. But Wilson's New Freedom reforms benefited both the general public and the corporations by balancing corporate interests and the well being of workers. To accomplish his goal, Wilson sought input from advisors representing big business, despite the fact that they were not in favor of any kind of regulation. This turned out to be a good strategy; the government was able to accomplish its goals, yet businesses believed they had protected their interests.

No Progressive agenda could succeed without reforming the nation's banking system, which had not been changed since the Civil War (1861–65). The Federal Reserve Act of 1913 established twelve Federal Reserve Banks to hold the reserve money of member banks across the United States. Member banks were nationally chartered banks that held stock in the new centralized Federal Reserve. The new U.S. banking authority stabilized the nation's monetary system and was overseen by the Federal Reserve Board. The Federal Reserve could create currency and expand or tighten credit by establishing interest rates. During World War I, the Federal Reserve made it possible for the United States to create new currency in order to finance war expenses. However, by doing this without a comparable increase in consumer goods and services, the inevitable result was economic inflation (an increase in the volume of money and credit that leads to a rise in prices of products and services). Wilson's administration believed controlling inflation was better than raising income taxes. Eventually, some taxes were raised to offset the costs of war.

The Federal Trade Commission threatened the interests of economically powerful men like John D. Rockefeller. Reproduced by permission of Archive Photos, Inc.

The first graduated federal income tax, imposed in 1913, was a means of replacing monies that previously had been gained through tariffs. Anyone with an annual income of $4,000 or more had to pay a percentage of his or her income to the federal government. That exempted most farmers and factory workers, who made less than $4,000 per year. Those who made between $4,000 and $20,000 paid 1 percent of their income to the government. There was a step increase for workers who made more than $20,000, and the maxi-

The Rockefeller Foundation Is Born

On May 14, 1913, John D. Rockefeller (1839–1937), oil entrepreneur and one of the founders of the modern corporation, donated $100 million to the Rockefeller Foundation. It was the single biggest philanthropic act in American history to that date. The Rockefeller Foundation was created, according to its charter, "to promote the well being of mankind throughout the world." Foundations such as the Rockefeller Foundation provide financial support for causes deemed worthy by the board of directors who oversee the distribution and management of a foundation's funds. Foundations also provide wealthy donors with tax-exempt ways to spend money on programs that they wish to support.

By the time Rockefeller retired from active work in the oil industry (circa 1890), he was making $10 million per year when the average American was earning $10 per week. At one time, Rockefeller earned 2.5 percent of the total national income.

mum tax was a payment of 6 percent by those who earned annual wages of more than $500,000. When the United States officially entered World War I in 1917 the government needed to raise more money to support the war effort. Congress passed the War Revenue Acts of 1917 and 1918. As a result of this legislation, the tax obligations of the wealthy increased, while low-wage earners and farmers still paid little or no income tax.

On the whole, the World War I years were advantageous to American industrial workers, whose wages rose substantially. For the wealthy, the purchase of war bonds resulted in profits; however, for the first time the rich endured substantial taxation on their incomes. The political and financial developments of the decade established a framework for twentieth-century American economics.

❖ THE MODERN FACTORY AND SYSTEMATIC MANAGEMENT OF LABOR

As the decade progressed, Americans were moving away from a rural, agricultural lifestyle of farming and self-employment in small enterprises in order to take steady-paying jobs in urban industrial plants. These modern factories were being run with new scientific techniques. The rise of the modern corporation and its factories was creating millions of new jobs in manufacturing industries that stressed the workers' reliance on machinery. Instead of a single foreman overseeing many employees who tended to work at their own pace, the newly designed plants relied on scientific studies of management and output. One of the most influential studies for efficiency in the modern, high-tech workplace was designed by a Philadelphia engineer, Frederick W. Taylor (1856–1915). His concept of "Taylorism" restructured the factory by measuring and extracting the maximum output for each worker with a stopwatch and time-and-motion studies. By these means he devised a work standard to match an hourly pay scale. For employees who succeeded in working above the set standard, there was higher pay. Taylor's studies were among the first notable scientific studies of efficiency in the corporate world. His work was followed by sophisticated efficiency studies by Frank Gilbreth (1868–1924) and Lillian Gilbreth (1878–1972), who set out to subdivide a worker's function into a series of necessary movements, thus avoiding extra exertion for the worker while providing maximum efficiency for the employer.

Meanwhile, Henry Ford (1863–1947) worked from 1910 through 1914 to formulate the most efficient means of building automobiles in a factory setting. Ford was a skilled mechanic who started the Ford Motor Company in the early twentieth century. In 1908, he introduced the Model T automobile to the public. It was Ford's intention to make as many Model Ts as possible in the most productive manner, in order to sell the maximum number of Model Ts at a price the public could afford. So great was the demand for motor cars that, between 1914 and 1916, the number sold in the United States tripled. The Ford Motor Company alone sold 730,041 cars between 1916 and 1917. Henry Ford pioneered the idea of mass production at his plant in Highland Park, Michigan. He did this with the assembly line, an arrangement of machines and laborers in which work passes from operation to operation until a completed product emerges.

In 1914, Ford instituted the "five-dollar day" at a time when the average daily wage was less than half that amount. Part of this was paid in regular wages, but in order to earn the full amount promised, workers were expected to meet standards of efficiency, maintain an acceptable lifestyle, and stay on the job for a set length of time, usually six months. Through a series of manuals that stressed what Ford called "Americanism," he encouraged sobriety, education, and clean living in the home. He guided many immigrant workers to U.S. citizenship through English lessons and other organized assimilation programs.

To oversee the progress of the workers, the Ford Motor Company established a Sociological Department that investigated the home life of

OPPOSITE PAGE
The first automatic conveyor belt production line was at the Ford Motor Company in Highland Park, Michigan.
Reproduced by permission of AP/Wide World Photos.

each Ford employee. If some aspect of an employee's marriage or domestic lifestyle did not meet Ford standards, then a portion of his wages would be withheld until the situation was corrected. Although the system was intrusive to the employees and expensive to run for the company, the results

The First African American Woman
to Become a Self-Made Millionaire

Sarah Breedlove "Madame C. J." Walker (1867–1919) began life as a most unlikely future millionaire. The daughter of former slaves, she was orphaned at the age of six. She married when she was fourteen and bore a daughter, A'Lelia, at seventeen. A few years later her husband was murdered. A widow at the age of twenty, Sarah worked as a cook and a housecleaner to support herself and her child.

In the early 1900s, Sarah Breedlove developed some hair products for her personal use. When she realized how few hair and beauty products were available for black women, she decided to market and sell her first three products: Wonderful Hair Grower, Glossine, and Vegetable Shampoo. In 1906, as the product sales were increasing steadily, she married Charles Joseph Walker. Soon she expanded her renamed line of "Madame C. J. Walker's" cosmetics and hair care products. In 1910, she established a manufacturing plant in Indianapolis, Indiana, for her beauty products; six years later, she opened an elegant beauty salon in Harlem, along with many Walker Schools of Beauty throughout the country.

In addition to being the first African American self-made woman millionaire, Walker became a major philanthropist and human rights activist. In 1917, she was part of a delegation that petitioned President Woodrow Wilson to make lynching a federal crime.

proved beneficial to both sides, for a while. At its core, the program favored workers of Anglo-Saxon heritage and discriminated against Eastern European and Middle Eastern immigrants, who not only had a hard time conforming to "Americanism" but were given the most dangerous jobs on the assembly line. Furthermore, African Americans and women were not hired by Ford until the outbreak of World War I, when jobs became harder to fill. During the war, the mood of the country changed, as Americans became more suspicious of blind authority, and Ford's program failed as disgruntled workers rejected the company's intrusions into their personal lives.

❖ THE RISE OF THE LABOR UNIONS

While the inhumanity of the assembly line served to diminish the self image of the worker, labor unions provided a way for an employee to regain a sense of worth. For a number of reasons, workers joined labor unions during the 1910s. They sought increased wages and job security through collective bargaining. They wanted to be a proud part of a community of workers. This was feeling that prevailed among employees at old-style factories, where human skills were more important than machinery. Unions also provided workers with education and recreation, including baseball teams, lectures, picnics, and dances; some even provided funerals when necessary.

One of the most influential of the era's union leaders was Samuel Gompers (1850–1924), who served as president of the American Federation of Labor (AFL) from 1886 to 1924. Although he asserted that the AFL was open to all workers, his organizing efforts focused on skilled workers in selected trades and excluded immigrants and female workers, at least during his period of leadership. A man with a practical approach to the concept of a union, Gompers kept the AFL on a mainstream course even when militant socialists tried to gain control of the union (socialists believed in the overthrow of the capitalist system and the distribution of all profits to the workers). Gompers allied his union with the Democratic Party, and he accepted several appointments to presidential advisory committees during World War I.

Just prior to the war, union leaders had difficulty attaining basic rights for their members, who seemed hopelessly vulnerable in modern factory settings. Entering the struggle was the Socialist Party and its dynamic leader, Eugene V. Debs (1855–1926). Debs led the Socialist-oriented International Workers of the World (IWW) into several bitter and violent strikes, first in Lawrence, Kansas, in 1912, and then in Paterson, New Jersey, and Akron, Ohio, the following year. The IWW membership focused on recruiting immigrants, women, and unskilled laborers: groups that the AFL deliberately excluded from its ranks. The government disapproved of the activities of the IWW, whose membership approached the one hundred thousand mark by late in the decade, because of the union's Socialist Party connections. From 1917 to 1921, Debs was imprisoned under the Espionage Act for his opposition to World War I. The Espionage Act had been passed to restrict any public or private activity

"Madame C. J." Walker was the first African American self-made woman millionaire. She developed and sold hair-care and beauty products exclusively for black women. **Courtesy of the Library of Congress.**

that the government classified as harmful to the United States during a time of war. Socialism was considered a dangerous political philosophy, therefore, the activities of groups and individuals who believed in socialist principles were monitored and restricted by the government.

Between 1917 and 1920, the AFL prospered as union membership in the United States increased by two million, reaching an all-time high of just over five million workers, or close to 20 percent of the American labor force. During the war, the AFL supported the government's policies and joined the federal crackdown on socialist groups. At the same time, the union won for its workers such concessions as the eight-hour workday and the right for labor to organize without fear of employers taking punitive action against them. The United Mine Workers was the largest union in the country, with five hundred thousand members. As the decade ended, even such powerful antiunion industries as meatpacking, steel, and the railroads were beginning to organize labor unions. After the war, however, the unions encountered less cooperation from the government. After the antilabor Republican Party took control of Congress in 1918, President Wilson was forced to pull back from his prolabor stance in an attempt to gain the cooperation of the legislators in approving the Treaty of Versailles, a multinational peace settlement drawn up in Versailles, France, after World War I. From then on, Wilson tempered his support of the unions, and for fifteen years after the war the power of the unions experienced a period of decline. Even the tough-minded AFL had to accept weaker labor-management relations.

Nevertheless, the unions remained active, flexing their muscle by calling 2,665 strikes—organized refusal to work—involving four million workers, in 1919. One of the year's principal protests was the national steel strike, which began with a concerted effort to sign up thousands of steelworkers as union members. After more than one hundred thousand steel laborers joined the union, a committee was formed to negotiate terms of employment with Elbert H. Gary (1846–1927), founder and chairman of the United States Steel Corporation. The group demanded increased salaries, an eight-hour workday, and the right to collective bargaining; otherwise, the union would strike on September 22. Even though President Wilson asked representatives of U.S. Steel to meet with the union spokesmen, Gary disregarded the demands. Then, he brought in thousands of strikebreakers (people to do the jobs of those participating in the strike) and deputized guards to break up union meetings. When the strike was called, 350,000 steelworkers in nine states walked off their jobs. In retaliation, police in several states attacked strikers who were holding peaceful meetings. A total of eighteen striking steelworkers were killed as federal and state troops attempted to break up picket lines.

To soothe public tensions, the steel companies ran a self-serving media campaign of newspaper advertisements, which put a pro-management face on the situation. To save their image, they depicted the labor action as a battle between the United States and a rabble-rousing gang of foreign revolutionaries. They portrayed the strikers as immigrant radicals seeking to bring down the American way of life. They also depicted the strikebreakers as African Americans and Hispanics, exploiting underlying prejudice along ethnic and racial lines. Soon, back-to-work movements formed among native-born Americans who wanted to save their jobs from foreign and minority elements, and the strike was called off in January 1920. It was a major defeat for the unions, but it was useful as a trial run for the union actions that would follow in the 1930s.

❖ WOMEN LABOR ORGANIZERS AND THE GARMENT INDUSTRY

By the late 1910s, the International Ladies' Garment Workers Union had 82,000 members and was one of the largest affiliates of the American

The interior of a New York City sweatshop. Unions were formed to make working conditions better for workers. **Reproduced by permission of the Corbis Corporation.**

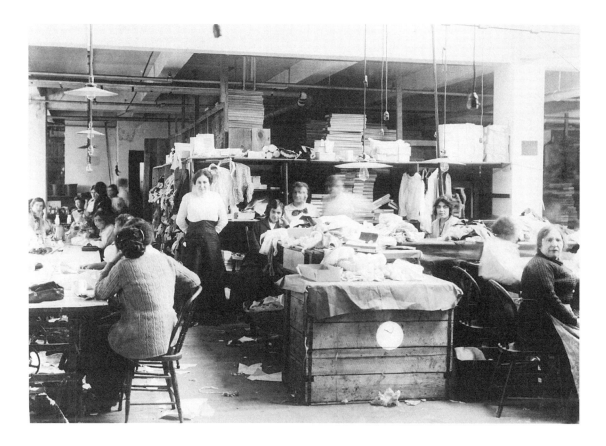

Triangle Shirtwaist Factory Fire

A fire swept the Triangle Shirtwaist Factory on the Lower East Side of Manhattan in New York City on March 25, 1911. One-hundred-forty-six women workers were killed when they were trapped in the cramped building that housed the sweatshop (a factory where people work long hours for little pay, usually in poor physical conditions). In the aftermath of the tragedy, laws were passed to improve building codes and the working conditions of factory workers. Despite the reforms, to this day, hazardous sweatshops and oppressive working conditions continue to be linked to the garment industry.

Federation of Labor (AFL). The fact that more than half the members were women is impressive, considering that the AFL shunned female membership. AFL president Samuel Gompers (1850–1924) and the majority of male union members viewed women as unworthy competitors for most industrial jobs, and saw them as casual workers who would quit their jobs as soon as they married. Throughout the decade, women had to struggle to make a place for themselves in the labor movement. Despite opposition, they pushed for the right to join unions and they aggressively sought leadership positions wherever they could. Middle-class female activists worked hand-in-hand with working women to create a strong alliance, one that was looked on with suspicion by many men.

One of the reasons that women were hired for factory jobs was their willingness to work for low wages in poor environments. When women began organizing for improved working conditions and higher salaries, their employers responded with harassment through police intervention and hired thugs. The company owners persuaded judges to levy fines against women for trumped-up infractions and for actions undertaken in pursuit of better working conditions. In 1910, women led strikes in the garment industries of New York City, Chicago, and Cleveland; they were defeated in violent skirmishes. Three years later, the women had much better results in four strikes, winning better pay and shorter hours. Among the strongest union activists were Jewish immigrants whose families had fought oppression in Eastern Europe. Agnes Nestor, Rose Schneiderman, Pauline Newman, Dorothy Jones, and Fannie Cohn were a few of the early labor organizers who encouraged female workers to unionize. Some of these leaders were members of the middle class and did not actu-

*The Triangle Shirtwaist
Company fire raised
awareness of the horrible
conditions that female
workers faced while on
the job.* **Reproduced by
permission of AP/Wide
World Photos.**

ally work in factories. Their involvement was questioned by some laborers who resented the emphasis they placed on educating workers about unionism and their advocacy of the women's suffrage (the right to vote) movement. Gompers himself questioned the participation of these women and was bothered by the growing number of socialists among them. During his leadership of the AFL, Gompers fought against the presence of women in both the union and the workplace in general.

❖ THE RISE OF THE RETAIL INDUSTRY

Twentieth-century America has been characterized as a society of consumers of mass-produced goods. By the early 1910s, U.S. factories had begun manufacturing an array of consumer goods, and President Wilson's success in lowering importation tariffs meant that items from many parts of the world were becoming available to the American public. Meanwhile, the advertising and public relations industries worked hard to persuade the public to buy and use all varieties of products. In 1910, businesses spent $600 million on advertising, which totaled 4 percent of the national income for that year. With such an emphasis on consumerism, if the department store had not yet existed, it would have had to have been invented!

In 1910, John Wanamaker (1838–1922), the creator of the modern department store, opened a twelve-story emporium in the heart of

Philadelphia. President William Howard Taft (1857–1930) led the dedication of the store in late 1911. Within this palatial structure, Wanamaker redesigned the retail sales business. This store was not only a place for customers to buy goods, it was also a fashioner of taste and style. Billboards with electric lights and colorful window displays brought potential customers into the store. Once inside, they were lured into buying products that represented modern trends in consumption, products chosen by professional buyers who scoured the world to bring customers the most appealing merchandise. Decorators used color, glass, and light to create a stress-free, enticing environment for shoppers, displaying goods as though the articles were priceless museum pieces. As women became more independent, the store tailored its campaigns to attract female shoppers. There were fashion shows to give customers a sense of the latest clothing styles and colors; a restaurant provided a place for weary customers to enjoy refreshments after a hard day of shopping. In the atrium sat the "Grand Court Console" theater organ, with its ten thousand pipes. Between 1911 and 1917, eight thousand additional pipes were added. Whether one wanted to purchase a dress pattern or a piece of fine Italian sculpture, Wanamaker's could satisfy the request. The store even boasted a Ford dealership!

Along with R. H. Macy's Herald Square store in New York City, Marshall Field's in Chicago, Dayton's in Minneapolis, and Filene's in Boston, all of which were built in the heart of major cities just after the turn of the twentieth century, John Wanamaker and Company pioneered techniques of advertising and selling practices for the modern department store. According to Wanamaker, "The time to advertise is all the time."

BOOKS

Gay, Kathlyn. *Who's Running the Nation? How Corporate Power Threatens Democracy.* New York: Franklin Watts, 1998.

Gilbreth, Frank B., Jr., and Ernestine Gilbreth Carey. *Belles on Their Toes.* New York: Bantam, 1984.

Gilbreth, Frank B., Jr., and Ernestine Gilbreth Carey. *Cheaper By the Dozen.* New York: Bantam, 1984.

Gilbreth, Lillian Moller. *As I Remember: An Autobiography by Lillian Gilbreth.* Norcross, GA: Engineering & Management Press, 1998.

Jeffrey, Laura. *Great American Businesswomen.* Springfield, NJ: Enslow Publishers, 1996.

Katz, William Loren. *Minorities in American History.* Vol. 4: *From the Progressive Era to the Great Depression, 1900–1929.* New York: Watts, 1974–75.

Laughlin, Rosemary. *John D. Rockefeller: Oil Baron and Philanthropist.* Greensboro, NC: Morgan Reynolds, 2001.

Lommel, Cookie. *Madame C. J. Walker.* Los Angeles: Melrose Square Publishing Company, 1993.

Meltzer, Milton: *Bread and Roses: The Struggle of American Labor, 1865–1915.* New York, Knopf, 1967.

O'Connell, Arthur J. *American Business in the Twentieth Century.* San Mateo, CA: Bluewood Books, 1999.

Skurzynski, Gloria. *Rockbuster.* New York: Atheneum Books, 2001.

Stewart, Gail. *1910s.* New York: Crestwood House, 1989.

Stone, Tanya Lee. *The Progressive Era and World War I.* Austin, TX: Raintree Steck-Vaughn, 2001.

Uschan, Michael V. *The 1910s.* San Diego, CA: Lucent Books, 1999.

Yannuzzi, Della A. *Madame C.J. Walker: Self-Made Businesswoman.* Berkeley Heights, NJ: Enslow Publishers, 2000.

WEB SITES

American Cultural History: The Twentieth Century, 1910–1919. http://www.nhmccd.cc.tx.us/contracts/lrc/kc/decade10.html (accessed on August 2, 2002).

General Motors Corporation Corporate History: 1910s. http://www.gm.com/company/corp_info/history/gmhis1910.html (accessed on August 2, 2002).

Samuel Gompers. http://www.pbs.org/joehill/faces/gompers.html (accessed on August 2, 2002).

chapter three *Education*

1910: **September** Dewey, Oklahoma, opens the nation's first nongraded school, where students in grades one to twelve work independently.

1911: The average cost of books per student enrolled in a public school is about $.78.

1911: Yearly tuition for college at Harvard is $150 per year; at Adelphi $180; at Colgate $60.

1911: Research shows that 60 percent of eighth graders in Hackensack, New Jersey, cannot write an "acceptable" composition on "A Day in My Life" in fifteen minutes.

1911: Rochester, New York, sets up a Bureau of Research and Efficiency to compile statistical information on public schools.

1912: A total of 2,569 students attend evening trade schools in New York City.

1912: The American Federation of Labor announces its stance that the technical and industrial education of workers should fall within the responsibility of the public school system.

1913: California begins to provide free elementary school books to every student.

1914: Harvard, Yale, Princeton, Columbia, and Cornell announce substantial increases in tuition. Harvard engineering students will pay $250, instead of the previous $150, for enrollment in a new cooperative program with the Massachusetts Institute of Technology (MIT).

1914: The Bureau of Education estimates the total cost of U.S. public education at $750 million. This figure is less than one-third the national expenditure for alcoholic beverages and only three times the amount paid for movie admissions that year.

1914: About one half of the nation's twenty million schoolchildren attend rural schools.

1915: Vermont adopts a junior-high-school plan, setting up one hundred separate buildings to house seventh through tenth graders.

1915: **September** The Supreme Court of Arkansas declares unconstitutional an enactment by the state legislature appropriating $50,000 of common school funds to build high schools.

1915: **December** In New York City, the American Association of University Professors (AAUP) is chartered, with John Dewey as its president.

1916: The American Federation of Teachers (AFT), a teacher-only labor union of the American Federation of Labor (AFL), is founded with John Dewey's assistance.

1916: A study in *School and Society* cites statistics to support its claim that the United States is endangered because not enough college-educated women are marrying.

1916: Many colleges include "The War Aims Course" in their curricula to explore issues involved in the Great War (later known as World War I).

1917: All the former slave states except Missouri and West Virginia have established county training schools for African American students.

1917: The Smith-Hughes Act provides federal funding to states to prepare students in trade, industry, home economics, and agriculture.

1917: At the New Trier Township High School in Winnetka, Illinois, a student council is formed to make and enforce school regulations, try pupils for infractions, and fix punishments.

1918: President Woodrow Wilson authorizes the U.S. Bureau of Education to assist state education officers in finding teachers for normal, secondary, and elementary schools due to a national emergency in teacher shortages.

1918: June 14 On Flag Day, "Americanization" meetings are held, urging the need to educate recent immigrants in American language, citizenship, and ideals.

1918: October The Federal Board of Vocational Education sends an appeal to disabled soldiers and sailors in hospitals to get educated in order to be able to lead independent lives after the war ends.

1919: John Dewey and his colleagues establish the New School for Social Research in New York City. It is an independent university run by the educators themselves.

1919: The Bureau of Education issues a bulletin on "Opportunities at College for Returning Soldiers," consisting of a list of institutions and facts about courses of study, tuition, and scholarships at each of the nation's colleges.

1919: January The Progressive Education Association is established. Members cite their dissatisfaction with the "inflexibilities" of traditional schools.

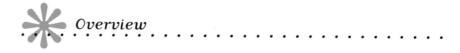

Overview

Before 1910, most American educators were influenced by European theories of education. As the economy in the United States changed from agrarian (farm-based) to industrial (factory-based), educators began to see that the European theories no longer fit the American lifestyle. To meet the growing needs in education, changes were made to ensure that public schooling would prepare students for an industrial society. Vocational instruction aimed at teaching practical work skills became a significant part of the American secondary school curriculum. With the support of corporations and business, public schools initiated programs to instruct young men and women on using modern machinery for industry and agriculture.

Teenagers were not the only group to benefit from vocational studies. For the first time, adults could learn about an array of vocational and academic subjects in evening extension courses and earn college credit through correspondence schools. Immigrants were offered courses in literacy and "Americanization." During and after World War I (1914–18), American soldiers and sailors were encouraged to complete high school degrees and enter colleges and universities.

In addition to curriculum adjustments to more closely connect education to the needs of the modern economy, there also were changes in the psychology of education. Educators such as John Dewey wanted to update teaching methods in public schools. Under the traditional teaching system, the instructor's job was to relate knowledge in a straightforward manner for students to memorize. Through the first ten years of the twentieth century, the teacher was viewed as an authoritarian figure who kept order in the classroom and tutored students in "the three Rs": reading, 'riting and 'rithmetic.

According to Dewey's system, which led to the development of a movement called progressive education, teachers would take a more humanistic approach to their students. The teacher, no longer a taskmaster but a guide, would encourage pupils to develop as human beings and show concern for their physical, mental, moral, and social growth. In 1916 the publication of Dewey's highly influential book, *Democracy and Education,* presented theories of modern educational psychology to a broad audience for the first time. Dewey's philosophies convinced people in powerful positions in government and industry, as well as educators, that progressive education was suitable for America's changing society.

In recognition of these new challenges for teachers, more sophisticated teacher training programs were developed during the decade. At the Teachers College at New York's Columbia University, a new curriculum was established that became a model for training programs across the nation. During the decade, not only teacher training, but also training for nurses, secretaries, homemakers, farmers, and factory workers, was refined and updated.

Not every school in the United States functioned with equal assets, however. Public schools in the South were impoverished. Often, schoolhouses were poorly lit and lacking indoor plumbing, and sometimes only a few books were available. A few of the Southern states had no compulsory education laws, which meant that even children too young to be needed for farming work were not legally required to attend school. Furthermore, school terms were shorter in the South than in other parts of the country. The lack of regulation fostered the problem of widespread child labor. Fortunately, throughout the decade, legislation was enacted that resulted in some uniform improvement in education for all parts of the United States.

At all levels of education, from public elementary schools to colleges and vocational training programs, racial and gender discrimination was evident. For instance, schools in the South were racially segregated (separated). If white students suffered from poor standards of education, their African American counterparts were even more deprived. Their school systems had poorly trained teachers, shorter terms, fewer books, and run-down schoolhouses. With the establishment of the National Association for the Advancement of Colored People (NAACP) and the advocacy of black intellectuals such as W.E.B. Du Bois, an effort was launched to raise the level of education for African Americans in the South.

Girls and women, too, were held back from pursuing certain kinds of higher education. Many colleges and universities did not accept applications from women. Particularly in professions such as the law and medicine, as well as theology, women held only a small number of positions. It was common belief in American society that women were best suited to be wives, mothers, and homemakers, and that they should *not* seek the jobs of men, who were considered the traditional breadwinners. In cases of racial and gender discrimination, the motivation for placing limitations on knowledge was the same: educating African Americans and women to a high academic level would encourage those groups to pursue equal rights with white men. Discrimination in education would remain a major issue for decades to come.

Felix Adler (1851–1933) Felix Adler advocated progressive education, calling for free kindergartens and vocational training. He held a professorship in Social and Political Ethics at Columbia University from 1902 until 1933. Adler was a strong proponent of educational, housing, and child labor reforms. In 1876, he founded the Ethical Culture Movement in New York City, which he helped to spread throughout the world. He planned a community founded on ethical living, rather than the worship of a supernatural deity, believing that ethical principles are not necessarily tied to philosophical or religious dogma (teachings). *Photo courtesy of the Library of Congress.*

Fannie Fern Phillips Andrews (1867–1950) From childhood, Fannie Fern Phillips Andrews wanted to teach. She graduated from the Salem (Massachusetts) Normal School, taught in the Boston school system for six years, and then received a degree in psychology and education from Radcliffe College in 1902. Andrews founded the American Peace League (later called the American School Citizenship League) in 1908 to promote peace and "international justice." It was her belief that those who could communicate and negotiate with persons different from themselves would avoid going to war to settle misunderstandings. From 1912 to 1921, she was active in the International Bureau of Education, which was formed according to her plan.

Charles Austin Beard (1874–1948) Historian Charles Austin Beard believed in free speech and self-expression. During his tenure as a Columbia University professor (1904–17), he maintained a strong stance on civil liberties. When several colleagues were dismissed for opposing the U.S. entry into World War I, Beard resigned his position. He later helped found the New School for Social Research. His most controversial publication came in 1913. In this work, titled *An Economic Interpretation of the Constitution of the United States,* Beard admired the wisdom of the authors of the Constitution but saw them as property owners who were safeguarding their own wealth, rather than representing the concerns of the majority. *Photo courtesy of the Library of Congress.*

Lucy Sprague Mitchell (1878–1967) After earning a degree in philosophy from Radcliffe College in 1900, Lucy Sprague Mitchell went on to become Dean of Women at the University of California, Berkeley. She was a forward-looking administrator who even encouraged sex hygiene instruction at a time when that was considered an inappropriate subject for classroom discussion. After moving to New York, she used a generous inheritance to found the Bureau of Educational Experiments, which became The Bank Street School of Education in 1950. Here, she implemented the theories of progressive education. She used intelligence tests with all students, including mentally retarded children, and masterminded innovations in early childhood education.

Robert Russa Moton (1867–1940) In 1890, Robert Russa Moton graduated from the Hampton Institute, an industrial school for African Americans in Virginia, and by 1893 became the institute's Commandant of Cadets, serving in that top administrative post until 1915. That year, he succeeded Booker T. Washington as principal of the Tuskegee Institute, and raised the curriculum from vocational to college level. He raised millions of dollars for black education and supervised the construction of hundreds of new school buildings. During World War I, Moton successfully defended black soldiers accused of a rape crime. In 1930, he was appointed to education commissions in Haiti and Liberia. *Photo reproduced by permission of Fisk University Library.*

Carter Godwin Woodson (1875–1950) In 1915, Carter Godwin Woodson established the Association for the Study of Negro Life and History in order to collect, preserve, and publish documents of the African American experience. At a time when black history was told with bias, if it was told at all, Woodson's work helped to create a scholarly record. The son of a former slave, Woodson grew up in poverty and did not attend high school until the age of twenty. Still, he went on to study at Berea College, the University of Chicago, the Sorbonne in Paris, and Harvard University, where he earned a doctorate in philosophy (Ph.D.) in 1912. *Photo reproduced by permission of the Corbis Corporation.*

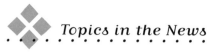

Topics in the News

❖ AMERICAN UNIVERSITIES DURING WORLD WAR I

When the United States entered World War I in 1917, a number of prominent educators recognized the conflict as a struggle between good and evil. Because much of the American educational system was based on British theories, the academic world naturally aligned with the Allied Powers (Great Britain, France, and Russia) against the Central Powers (Germany, Austria-Hungary, Ottoman Turkey, and Bulgaria). So strong was the support for the war among educators that the *New Republic* magazine editors labeled the conflict "the thinking man's war." The article continued, "College professors, headed by a President [Woodrow Wilson (1856–1924)] who himself is a former professor, contributed more effectively to the decision to go to war than did farmers, businessmen, or politicians."

A few college professors became actively involved in the war effort. For example, Harvard chemistry scholar James Conant (1893–1978) began researching the production of poison gas for use against the enemy, as well as the development of gas masks to protect our own soldiers from the fumes. In 1917, the editor of *National History Review* established the National Board for Historical Service in order to spread ideas in support of the war through academic lectures and articles. History professors organized a lecture bureau, which provided people qualified to speak about the war effort at high school commencements, teacher training sessions, and similar occasions. The group also edited informational booklets on war topics, published a book of war-related poetry, and sponsored essay contests for students and teachers.

Academics volunteered to work for the Committee on Public Information (CPI), a group set up by the government to publicize official war policy and give the American public "the feeling of partisanship that comes with full, frank statements concerning the conduct of the public business." Many important scholars wrote tracts and public announcements for the CPI. Still, the group's main intention was to spread the ideas of President Wilson and his administration as propaganda (material designed to favor one viewpoint) rather than as unbiased academic documents. In fact, a number of scholars working for the CPI translated foreign language newspaper editorials and accounts of the war. Through this process, the CPI and its scholars were determined to catch foreign subversives who might be publishing opinions in opposition to the U.S. government.

By early 1918, 157 campuses had instituted military training programs for student-soldiers. Colleges and universities, as well as technical and trade schools, began teaching radiotelegraphy, automobile repair, and sheet metal work to nonacademic drafted men. Many young men who were enrolled as college students also received military training. As a result of the Morrill Act of 1862, all land-grant schools were required to prepare their male students for war. By the fall of 1918, all universities offered military training under the auspices of the War Department. On October 1 of that year, 140,000 students at 516 schools were inducted into the Students' Army Training Corps (SATC). They would not be called into active service until they received their degrees or turned twenty-one, whichever came first. Many officer candidates and technical experts were groomed on university campuses.

The academic podium had long been a soapbox for free speech, but this situation changed when the United States entered into the war. No longer did college administrators tolerate radical opinions. Dissenters were dismissed from academic positions. In June 1917, Nicolas Murray Butler (1862–1947), president of Columbia University, declared, "What had been tolerated has become intolerable now. What had been wrong-headedness was now sedition [revolt against lawful authority]. What had been folly was now treason." It would be many years before the campus paranoia that led to such disturbing closed-mindedness was replaced by the freedom of expression more traditionally linked to university life.

❖ THE EMERGENCE OF THE MODERN UNIVERSITY

Universities such as Johns Hopkins and the University of Chicago pioneered the concept that upper-level schools should not only pass along the best of traditional knowledge, but also encourage the creation of new knowledge through scholarship and research. Another modern notion about education, that the state was obliged to provide higher education to all citizens, originated in Michigan and Wisconsin. The quality of Michigan's institutes of higher learning was ensured by revenues from state taxes. The University of Wisconsin took its responsibility to the state literally, developing educational programs that helped provide expert knowledge to leaders and workers in agriculture, as well as forestry, utilities, banking, railroads, and government. The University of Wisconsin, the University of Michigan, Columbia University, and Pennsylvania State College were among the first schools to sponsor extension programs to make higher education available to tens of thousands more people than the .05 percent of the population who were then enrolled in colleges or universities.

During this decade, adults who had not had the advantage of full-time university study could now attend lectures and participate in correspondence schools for academic credit. The new, broader availability of higher education would bring important changes to those without the money or family connections needed to pursue a college education. Previously, most people could expect to earn no more than high school diplomas. Now they could obtain bachelor degrees through extension programs and other alternatives designed for working adults, qualifying themselves for more interesting jobs and higher wages, and increasing their knowledge of fields of study such as science, business, literature, and mathematics.

❖ PROGRESSIVE EDUCATION AND EDUCATION REFORM

The philosophies of progressive education, which encouraged a humanistic, developmental approach to teaching and learning, had its roots in many separate theories about the emotional and physical well-being of the child. Progressive education's principal representative in the United States had been Francis Parker (1837–1902), who founded schools in the late nineteenth century to teach a flexible curriculum and self-expression to children, instead of traditional subjects. It was John Dewey (1859–1952), however, who set down formal, intellectual foundations for progressive education. Many of the methods of progressive education were taught at the Teachers College at Columbia University during the tenure (1909–30) of one of its leading advocates, William Heard Kilpatrick (1871–1965). One of Dewey's disciples, Kilpatrick is known as the father of progressive education.

In 1919, a group of educators gathered in Washington, D.C., to found the Progressive Education Association (PEA). They believed that children should develop naturally with freedom for initiative and self-expression in an interesting environment. They also believed that children should have a genuine interest in their studies. Teachers were to be guides, not taskmasters. They were to be aware of the physical health of pupils and make sure the children learned in wholesome and healthful environments. Teachers were to maintain scientific studies of their pupils to ensure each child's development. Progressive schools were designed to operate in cooperation with parents to fulfill the child's needs. These schools provided leadership in educational movements, and were laboratories for new ideas as well as the best of traditional methods.

Progressive education continued well after World War I (1914–18). As it evolved, some schools exaggerated the freedom and creativity of the movement and ran excessively permissive programs that were soundly criticized by Dewey.

For most of the 1910s, the normal school (a two-year institution that trained teachers) was the most common training program for elementary school teachers, and even for rural high school teachers in certain states.

The Ideal Teacher...Circa 1917

In 1917, the superintendent of schools in Port Chester, New York, published the following portrait of the ideal teacher:

Voice: should be well modulated, clear and winning with correct pronunciation and wide vocabulary.

Manners: should be that of cultured ladies and gentlemen.

Conduct: should possess a character indicated by irreproachable actions reflecting high ideals and purposes.

Work Habits: should be systematic, accurate, prompt, cheerful, and masterful in thought and action.

Self Control: should reflect ease, poise, and a judicial and thoughtful attitude.

Inspirational Force: should be strong in encouraging thought-provoking, ambition-arousing, growth-promoting, and success-inspiring action.

Leadership: should be evident in all actions.

Executive Ability: should display initiative and resourceful action.

Cooperation: should be loyal, frank, kind, sympathetic, and helpful.

Common Sense: should display this in refusing to gossip, in conforming to the customs of the community, and in a saving sense of humor.

Attitude: should be optimistic, enthusiastic, respecting the superintendent, trusting the principal, liking associates, loving pupils, while smiling, and radiating good cheer.

Source: Elmer Redmund, "Teaching Efficiency," *American School Board Journal,* 51 (March 1917): p. 45.

A person who had completed two years of high school could enroll in a two-year normal school to learn basic academic subjects, review topics covered in elementary schools, and then practice teach under the supervision of an experienced teacher. However, throughout the decade, education theorists were adjusting the teacher's role from an adult who simply imparted knowledge to a developmentally oriented guide who helped each student learn individually. As a result, more sophisticated training became necessary, so colleges began offering four-year teacher training programs. With the Teachers College at Columbia University leading the way, many institutes of higher learning developed well-rounded, diverse programs to prepare teachers according to progressive education principles. By 1920, 450 colleges offered four-year teacher education degrees.

During World War I, U.S. military personnel responses to survey questions about education prompted educators to step up reform programs. Statistics showed that in the Midwest, fewer than 10 percent of the teachers had more than two years of high school education. The surveys noted high levels of physical defects among the soldiers, indicating the need for health education in rural schools. Responses also brought to light high levels of illiteracy among people who were born in the United States, and special literacy problems among immigrants. These surveys provided a significant opportunity to re-evaluate the level of education in the country. Recognizing that such problems existed in U.S. education proved to be the catalyst for increased education reforms in the 1920s.

❖ VOCATIONAL EDUCATION

As farmers added machinery to their farming procedures and factory workers encountered the tools of modern industry, the need for special training became clear. Most workers could look at a rake or a hammer and figure out its proper usage. When it came to motor-driven machinery and specialized agricultural and industrial implements, however, workers needed more than a salesman's demonstration or even a typed manual to learn to operate them safely. The total value of agriculture products was less than $5 billion in 1900 but grew to almost $8.5 billion by 1910. By 1919 farm products totaled close to $12.5 billion. This growth was due to the increased use of farm machinery.

Throughout the 1910s, public schools became increasingly responsible for vocational training. In earlier years, young people had been apprenticed to experienced workers known as journeymen in order to receive on-the-job training. That system fell apart with the growth of labor unions, which placed formal limits on the number of apprentices a company could hire. It was left to the public schools to take up the slack in vocational training. Particularly in the North, schools developed cooperative education programs that combined studies in conventional academic subjects with vocational instruction. These programs were often supported by major industries and retailers such as General Electric, department store magnate John Wanamaker, Sears Roebuck, and National Cash Register. These companies knew the importance of helping young people to learn trades related to every field of business and industry.

Agricultural training began expanding in the early 1910s. Not surprisingly, the areas in the forefront of this movement were the farming regions of the Midwest. Wisconsin led the way with the establishment of tuition-free, two-year county schools that taught farming and home economics. Soon, additional schools opened across the country. By 1915, 4,665 high schools were offering agriculture courses. Such programs were spurred on by the Smith-Lever Act of 1914, which offered federal dollars for extension courses in agriculture and home economics. The Smith-Hughes Act followed in 1917, granting funds directly to schools for the teaching of agricultural, industrial, and commercial courses. By the close of the decade, the federal government made available $3 billion for the training and salaries of vocational teachers, federal supervisory tasks, and research about vocational education. The money was dispensed to the states by the Federal Board for Vocational Education (FBVE).

As in agriculture, the business sector of the economy was growing more complex. Students who intended to enter the world of commerce by taking jobs in department stores, banks, and offices needed special train-

Vocational classes taught farmers how to use newly developed machinery.

ing to operate new machinery and work with more sophisticated business systems. To meet the need, school systems in major cities began setting up secondary commercial schools, some with five-year programs, to prepare pupils for the business world. Courses were given in stenography (writing in shorthand), bookkeeping, and business English. By 1918, high schools around the nation reported 278,275 students were studying commercial education curricula.

❖ SPECIAL SCHOOLING FOR WOMEN

The majority of secondary schools in the 1910s offered three curriculum options for young women: academic studies, home economics, and teacher training. The U.S. Bureau of Education announced in its 1917 to 1918 *Biennial Survey of Education* that 73 percent of girls enrolled in secondary schools opted to take the academic course, while 10 percent chose home economics, and a mere 2 percent were preparing to be teachers. John Dewey and other progressive educators were designing education programs for females with an eye toward their future participation in the community. On the other hand, conservative groups feared that secondary education for young women could lead them away from marriage, home-making, and child-rearing. What was clear to both conservatives and progressives was the fact that young women were making up a large percentage of the high school population. In 1918, 57.9 percent of secondary school students were female.

The home economics movement, fueled by federal grants through the Smith-Lever Act of 1914 and the Smith-Hughes Act of 1917, emphasized the agricultural lifestyle. Young women were taught how to grow fresh vegetables in gardening clubs and then learned to can the vegetables they had raised. In 1918, the U.S. Bureau of Education reported that home economics courses were growing at a rate of one thousand per year in public schools. Courses such as cooking and sewing became mandatory for girls in upper-level elementary school grades, and were electives for secondary school students. By 1919, young women were able to spend school time in model apartments and child-care centers, where they learned many aspects of keeping house and raising children firsthand.

Attending college was an unrealistic goal for all but a very few female high school graduates. Those who were able to study beyond secondary school often attended business colleges to become secretaries and book-keepers, or they enrolled in normal schools for teacher training. Those who were able to attend liberal arts colleges and universities were from the wealthy or upper middle class. In the early twentieth century, the number of women on college campuses rose substantially, from 32,485 in 1898 to

Women on college campuses during the 1910s often considered them-selves to be "new women," who were freed from traditional roles by recent social reforms. In some ways, they foreshadowed the "flappers" of the Jazz Age. As late as 1907, when men were allowed to attend dances at women's colleges, couples were only supposed to walk to the music. A man and a woman were forbidden from dancing together. Then several women at Smith College rose up against the system and danced "the forbidden waltz" with their male guests. By 1913, certain couple dances were permitted at colleges across the country. An untamed dance such as the "turkey trot" was banned at Barnard College in 1915, and the tango remained on the forbidden list at a number of Midwestern campuses. In 1912, a male graduate school student at the University of Chicago lambasted tango dancing: "This wriggling will soon lead to a nervous breakdown for innocent girls."

Source: Barbara Miller Solomon, *In the Company of Educated Women* (New Haven, Yale University Press, 1985), pp. 102–04.

128,677 in 1919. Still, many colleges persisted in not allowing women to enroll, particularly schools in the South, and many postsecondary schools attended by women were for females only.

Besides teaching and secretarial work, another typical vocation for women was nursing. During the 1910s, nursing education was being formalized in order to attract more highly educated women. The physical damage done to so many soldiers in the war demonstrated the need for trained nurses. Medical science was in a period of growth as well. To provide the resources for nursing students to acquire this growing body of theoretical and scientific knowledge, major colleges and universities began to develop nursing departments. By the close of the decade, sixteen leading universities had organized their own nursing programs, and another fourteen had established affiliations with nursing schools. Twelve universities even had graduate studies programs in nursing. By 1920, 54,953 women were enrolled in nursing degree programs.

Throughout the decade women had only very limited access to jobs in medicine, law, theology, or higher education. These professions were considered suitable only for men. Young women were discouraged from pursuing these careers, and when they actually did successfully attain positions as doctors, lawyers, clergy leaders, or professors, they were often criticized for taking jobs away from men. Many colleges prohibited women from applying for legal or medical degrees. Even so, in 1919, 888 women were enrolled in medical courses, 1,171 in law courses, and 874 in theology courses.

❖ SOUTHERN SCHOOLS AND SEGREGATION

In general, schooling in the South was lower in quality than in the rest of the country. In 1910, the average annual school term in the region lasted only 121 days, and no compulsory attendance laws were in existence. As the decade progressed, improvements were made to establish a longer school year, compulsory attendance through eighth grade, and higher wages for white teachers. In 1915, an average of $8.50 was spent on each child in a southern school, compared to $22.19 per child in the North. That was a marked improvement from the turn of the twentieth century, when only $3.00 per child was spent per year in the South. On the whole, Southern colleges and universities also lagged behind the rest of the country in budget expenditures and overall quality of education.

The South was the poorest section of the country, and its education system was a reflection of its economic condition. During the 1910s, steps were taken to attempt to better educate the southern population. For instance, laws limiting and prohibiting child labor were enacted throughout the South from 1904 to 1918. Once children were no longer a legal source of cheap labor, compulsory school attendance laws could be implemented and enforced.

According to the U.S. census of 1910, 90 percent of the African American population resided in the South. While all southern schools suffered from the problems of the region, African American students bore the heaviest burden of the impoverished system. Black students and white students were segregated, or separated by race, in their schools. Black public schools remained open only three to four months per year, and minority teachers were paid only $17 to $25 per month. This was less than the salaries of black convicts.

OPPOSITE PAGE
A southern rural school for blacks in 1915 is just one example of how African American students bore the heaviest burden of the South's impoverished education system.

Prior to the 1910s, African American educator Booker T. Washington (1856–1915) and his Tuskegee (Alabama) Institute had established a system of industrial education for blacks. Students worked in manual jobs to help pay for their training, which emphasized learning a trade and building character. Opposing Washington was a group of people who formed the National Association for the Advancement of Colored People (NAACP) in 1910. The NAACP stood for political equality and civil rights for blacks; in their view, Washington's emphasis on industrial education was not in the best interests of people of color.

In 1911, African American intellectual W.E.B. Du Bois (1868–1963) wrote that Washington was leading black people backward into slavery

with his limited model of education. The controversy was, perhaps, over the question of whether or not *some* career education and training was better than *nothing* for a minority population with few job opportunities. Washington relied on funding from northern white philanthropists to

keep his own school running, and he realized that state and federal aid would be needed to improve the quality of African American public schools. Yet he undoubtedly knew that if African Americans ever became well educated, they would be likely to demand more civil rights—rights that all-white legislatures in the North and the South were not likely to grant them. Washington believed that such an upheaval would limit the northern support on which the Tuskegee Institute depended and result in a backlash against educated African Americans. Despite the growing movement of black intellectuals to raise standards and conditions in their public schools in the South, the inferior, segregated system would keep training southern blacks mainly for industrial vocations and dole out limited education, in general, for decades to come.

For More Information

BOOKS

Bloom, Harold, ed. *W.E.B. Du Bois*. Philadelphia: Chelsea House, 2001.

Haskins, James. *Separate, but Not Equal: The Dream and the Struggle*. New York: Scholastic, 1998.

Kessler-Harris, Alice. *Women Have Always Worked: A Historical Overview*. New York: Feminist Press at the City University of New York, 1981.

Lusane, Clarence. *The Struggle for Equal Education*. New York: Franklin Watts, 1992.

McDaniel, Melissa. *W.E.B. Du Bois: Scholar and Civil Rights Activist*. New York: Franklin Watts, 1999.

Rhym, Darren. *The NAACP*. Philadelphia: Chelsea House, 2001.

WEB SITES

American Cultural History: The Twentieth Century, 1910–1919. http://www.nhmccd.cc.tx.us/contracts/lrc/kc/decade10.html (accessed on August 2, 2002).

The Two Nations of Black America. http://www.pbs.org/wgbh/pages/frontline/shows/race/etc/road.html (accessed on August 2, 2002).

OPPOSITE PAGE
The Tuskegee Institute, established by Booker T. Washington, provided industrial education for African Americans.
Reproduced by permission of the Corbis Corporation.

Government, Politics, and Law

1910: **March 26** Congress amends the Immigration Act of 1907, prohibiting criminals, anarchists, the poor, and people carrying infectious disease from entering the United States.

1910: **June 20** Congress authorizes the New Mexico Territory and the Arizona Territory to form state governments and apply for statehood.

1910: **June 25** Congress passes the Publicity Act, requiring members of Congress to report campaign contributions.

1911: **May 29** In *U.S.* v. *American Tobacco Company,* the Supreme Court finds "the tobacco trust" in violation of the Sherman Antitrust Act.

1912: **January 6** New Mexico becomes the forty-seventh state.

1912: **February 14** Arizona becomes the forty-eighth state.

1912: **April 14** The new luxury ocean liner *Titanic* hits an iceberg and sinks within hours. The investigation that follows attracts international attention.

1912: **May 12** The national convention of the Socialist Party of America convenes in Indianapolis. Eugene V. Debs is the presidential nominee.

1913: **February 25** The Sixteenth Amendment is adopted, legalizing a federal income tax.

1913: **March 4** Woodrow Wilson takes the oath of office and becomes the twenty-eighth U.S. president.

1913: **December 23** The Federal Reserve Act becomes law. It establishes a regulatory system to increase economic stability throughout the country.

1914: **July 28** Austria declares war on Serbia in what will later become known as World War I.

1914: **September 26** The Federal Trade Commission is set up to prevent monopolies and preserve competition and free commerce.

1915: **January 28** Congress establishes the U.S. Coast Guard.

1915: **May 7** A British passenger liner, the *Lusitania,* is sunk by Germans off the Irish coast. Among the dead are 128 Americans.

1916: Margaret Sanger, a prominent advocate of birth control, is found guilty of obscenity charges in New York State for distributing her book *Family Limitation* (1914).

1916: **January 27** President Wilson begins a tour of the United States urging Americans to prepare for their nation's entry into the war in Europe.

1916: **July 11** Congress passes the Federal Highway Act, authorizing assistance to states for road construction.

1916: **September 7** Congress passes the Workmen's Compensation Act, which offers coverage to five hundred thousand federal workers.

1917: **February 3** The United States severs diplomatic relations with Germany.

1917: **March 5** President Wilson is inaugurated for his second term in office.

1917: **March 20** Wilson's cabinet unanimously advises the president to ask Congress to declare war on Germany.

1917: **November 6** An amendment to the New York State constitution gives women the right to vote in state elections.

1918: Mississippi becomes the last state to pass a law authorizing compulsory school attendance.

1918: **January 8** President Wilson addresses Congress to present the Fourteen Points, his proposal for peace for a postwar world.

1918: **March 19** Congress passes legislation to put into effect Daylight Saving Time, a step to conserve energy in wartime.

1918: **August 16** U.S. troops are dispatched to Siberia to aid the White Russian Army. They are withdrawn in April 1920.

1918: **November 3** The Allies sign an armistice with Austria-Hungary.

1918: **November 11** On the eleventh hour of the eleventh day of the eleventh month of 1918, the armistice ending World War I goes into effect.

1918: **December 4** President Wilson sails for France to attend the Paris Peace Conference. The French people welcome him enthusiastically.

1919: The national debt rises from $2 billion in 1917 to $26 billion in 1919.

1919: **January 29** The Eighteenth Amendment, banning the transportation and sale of alcoholic beverages, is ratified.

1919: **February 14** President Wilson proposes the League of Nations at the Paris Peace Conference.

1919: **March 15** Units of the American Expeditionary Forces organize the American Legion.

1919: **June 28** The Treaty of Versailles is signed, officially ending World War I.

1919: **August 14** In a highly publicized trial, the *Chicago Tribune* is found guilty of having libeled Henry Ford by calling the industrialist an anarchist.

1919: **November 19** The U.S. Senate fails to ratify the Treaty of Versailles, making membership in the newly established League of Nations all but impossible.

Overview

During the 1910s, a number of highly determined interest groups pushed for changes and reforms in government, politics, and law, making the decade one of social and political turbulence. The political elections reflected the dynamics of the period. Former U.S. President Theodore Roosevelt (1858–1919) once again threw his wide-rimmed hat into the presidential race in 1912 and split the Republican Party into two factions. As a result, a relatively inexperienced politician, Democrat Woodrow Wilson (1856–1924), was elected to the country's highest office. For much of the decade, Wilson's administration was able to enact legislation effectively through a supportive, Democrat-dominated Congress. With the 1918 elections, however, both the Senate and House majorities were handed to the Republicans. Without congressional support, Wilson's ability to transfer his political philosophies into law ended. Particularly in 1919, the president's carefully drawn plans for international peace were taken up by European leaders but stifled in the United States by party politics.

The United States became involved in international politics mainly through "dollar diplomacy," which was a form of political-economic intervention. With U.S. banks and businesses dispersed throughout Latin America and the Caribbean, the American government either supported or squelched leadership in these regions, based on how American investments were affected by those in power in any given place or time. Relations with Mexico, in particular, were strained throughout the 1910s. Through the power of the dollar, the United States became a world power as the decade progressed.

From 1914 through 1918, The Great War—known later as World War I—was raging in Europe, and for almost three years, the United States managed to stay out of the conflict. However, by 1917 world events, particularly Germany's initiation of unrestricted submarine warfare, compelled the United States to enter the war alongside Great Britain, France, and Russia, against Germany and Austria-Hungary, which were also aligned with Ottoman Turkey and Bulgaria. America quickly prepared for entry into the conflict by building up war-related industries. The government was soon developing an army trained for perilous trench warfare.

As the economy developed and became more compartmentalized, so did America's political factions. Farmers, laborers, industrialists, educators, social workers, and scientists all called for laws to benefit their aims. Minorities, too, protested to gain equal voices in society: Women's groups pushed for voting rights, while African Americans fought for the civil rights that had been denied them through "Jim Crow Laws" (Southern laws that kept blacks separated from whites).

Youngsters being exploited through unregulated child labor practices needed representation. Reformers had published exposes of the brutal treatment of children in factories and mines, but change was coming very slowly. As early as 1890, social activist Jacob Riis documented the miserable conditions of child laborers dwelling in New York City tenements, including widespread illiteracy and no access to schooling. During the 1910s, there was some progress on this issue, especially since the public began to see education as a means toward creating good citizens.

The attitude toward workers' compensation changed as the decade advanced. In 1910, workers injured on the job were considered to be responsible for their predicaments. The only way workers could pursue compensation was to sue their employers. By the end of the decade, many employers began to carry insurance against on-the-job injuries, and legislation was helping to set up standardized workers' compensation. Meanwhile, certain industries began investing in safer equipment to make on-the-job injuries less apt to occur.

Important legislation of the decade involved morality. The most explosive enactment of the period was the ratification of the Eighteenth Amendment in 1919, which prohibited the sale and transportation of alcoholic beverages. Under Prohibition the nation went "dry," meaning that alcoholic beverages were no longer legally available, but this situation ultimately spawned an illegal trade in intoxicating liquors that lasted until the amendment was repealed in 1933. Other morality-charged legislation involved regulation of narcotics and illegal medicines. Also the sensationalized, though real, practice of white slave trafficking (abducting young innocent women for the purpose of prostitution) was made a felony through the enactment of The Mann Act.

Newton D. Baker (1871–1937) As U.S. secretary of war from 1916 to 1921, Newton D. Baker handled the challenging task of mobilizing U.S. troops for the war against Germany. Baker's first significant duty was to send U.S. troops under General John J. Pershing into Mexico to capture revolutionary Pancho Villa. A pacifist, Baker was slow to develop U.S. military forces. In late 1917, his efforts were the focus of a congressional investigation, under allegations that the military build-up was being done in an inefficient manner; his work was eventually praised, however. From 1912 to 1915, Baker was mayor of Cleveland, where he instituted tax reforms and curtailed the power of utility companies. *Photo courtesy of the Library of Congress.*

Louis D. Brandeis (1856–1941) A millionaire before he reached the age of fifty, Louis D. Brandeis chose to sideline a successful career in corporate law to become an associate justice of the Supreme Court. He served with distinction in this capacity from 1916 until his retirement in 1939. The son of Jewish immigrants, he graduated from Harvard Law School and went on to become a tireless advocate for public interest issues such as labor reform. His liberal stance in law cases made him a target of Republican conservatives who labeled him an advocate of "radicalism." In the decades succeeding Brandeis's tenure on the Supreme Court, many of his decisions have come to be considered landmarks. *Photo reproduced by permission of the Corbis Corporation.*

Oliver Wendell Holmes Jr. (1841–1935) Oliver Wendell Holmes Jr. served as an associate justice on the Supreme Court from 1902 to 1932. While he wrote dissenting opinions in only seventy of six thousand cases, Holmes is remembered as "the great dissenter" for the significance of those opinions. He viewed the law as an evolving process and veered from the style of justice by which precedent dictates the only permissible decision. Instead, he believed that the U.S. Constitution was the framework by which the important issues of the day should be judged and addressed. He was among the first to acknowledge the government's move towards intervention in all facets of national life.

Edward M. House (1858–1938) As President Woodrow Wilson's adviser on European affairs during the years leading up to and during World War I, Edward M. House was one of the most influential men in America. He was instrumental in helping Wilson get elected in 1912, and then he helped the president choose his cabinet members. Prior to his political career, House managed his father's cotton plantations, which he eventually inherited; House's decision to sell the properties made him independently wealthy. At the end of the war, he gathered together a group of intellectuals and foreign policy experts known as "The Inquiry," who drafted policy for an international peace. *Photo courtesy of the Library of Congress.*

John J. Pershing (1860–1948) U.S. General John J. Pershing commanded the American Expeditionary Forces (AEF) during World War I. He previously had distinguished himself by leading forces into Mexico in 1916 and 1917 in an effort to capture Mexican revolutionary Pancho Villa (1878–1923) after his 1916 attack on Columbus, New Mexico. Pershing failed to track him down, but his efforts did serve to diminish Villa's power. Pershing's competence and determination was rewarded with his appointment, by President Woodrow Wilson, to a key military leadership position during the war. In September 1919, Pershing was named general of the armies, the highest rank in the U.S. Army. He also was army chief of staff from 1921 to 1924. *Photo courtesy of the Library of Congress.*

Woodrow Wilson (1856–1924) Woodrow Wilson was U.S. president from 1913 to 1921. He tried to keep the United States from becoming involved in world conflicts during the mid-1910s but during his second term in office, he realized it would be necessary to prepare America for the country's inevitable entry into "The Great War," now known as World War I (1914–18). After seeing the United States through the war, Wilson attended the Paris Peace Conference in 1919 and was a significant contributor to the terms of international peace. His plan was called the Fourteen Points. It included the establishment of the League of Nations as an institution to negotiate future conflicts. While the plan was not successful at the time, it was a precursor to the creation of the United Nations in 1945. Wilson began his political career in 1910, as the governor of New Jersey. As a young man, he had been a lawyer. Before entering politics, Wilson was a college professor and administrator, and served as president of Princeton University. *Photo reproduced by permission of AP/Wide World Photos.*

❖ ❖ *Topics in the News* . . . .

❖ AMERICA AND WORLD AFFAIRS: DOLLAR DIPLOMACY

During the 1910s, the United States left its position of self-imposed isolationism to become a world economic and political power, a role that previously had been held by European nations. Much of America's power was sought and achieved through the international marketplace. Starting with the presidency of William Howard Taft (1857–1930) and continuing through the administrations of Woodrow Wilson (1956–1924), U.S. intervention in world affairs took the forms of military action and, most often, social-economic involvement. The establishment of political relations with foreign nations through economic trade or support became known as dollar diplomacy. As Taft stated in his final message to Congress on December 3, 1912, foreign policy should include "substituting dollars for bullets." Those who favored dollar diplomacy praised America's intervention into foreign politics as a means of promoting democracy and economic growth. Critics described it as a policy of self-interest only, and an economic form of imperialism (the extension of a nation's power through the acquisition and direct control of land or territories). Through the practice of dollar diplomacy in Latin America and the Caribbean, where American banks and businesses were often protected with an onsite American military presence, the United States became a nation of influence in the world.

Since the 1800s, the Caribbean had been a strategic region for American naval domination. Caribbean, Latin American, and U.S. interests were intertwined. Between 1910 and 1916, the U.S. government dispatched troops to Cuba, Haiti, Mexico, Nicaragua, and elsewhere to oversee its interests. If the U.S. government did not trust or have good international business relations with the prime political leader in one of these countries, it typically helped rebel factions within the country to defeat him. In some cases, the federal government saw to it that "puppet regimes," governments that were under the economic and political control of the United States, were established in foreign countries to obligate those governments to do business with U.S. banks.

In 1915, U.S. troops were deployed to the capital city of Port-au-Prince, Haiti, after native Haitians killed General Vilbrun Guillaume Sam, a repressive dictator who had just assassinated 167 political prisoners. Americans set up a puppet government in Haiti and soon were in full control of its police force, public works department, and economy. These steps were taken to secure the assets of the National City Bank of New York in Haiti. During the U.S. occupation of Haiti, civil liberties of

Haitians were curtailed, but only a portion of a $16 million loan promised to them by the National City Bank was ever disbursed.

In at least one case, the United States gained control of foreign properties without the aid of troops, simply by using the power of the checkbook. On August 4, 1916, the United States purchased 68 small Caribbean islands—133 square miles, called the Virgin Islands—from Denmark. The cost was $25 million.

❖ AMERICA AND WORLD AFFAIRS: THE MEXICAN REVOLUTION

Throughout the decade, America was drawn into the unsettled politics of its neighbor to the south. The Mexican government had long been in shambles. Porfirio Diaz (1830–1915), who ruled Mexico from 1876 to 1911, suppressed uprisings with violence and kept his elected office through corrupt election processes. Under his rule, the Mexican peasant class lived miserable lives. His opponent in 1910 was Francisco Madero (1873–1913), a rich man who promised all the Mexican people better lives. Madero was imprisoned by Diaz, but he escaped to the United States, where he formed an army and returned to Mexico to defeat Diaz. On May 25, 1911, Diaz fled to Paris. Once he became Mexico's president, Madero broke his promises and ran the government in a corrupt manner.

Next, Victoriano Huerta (1854–1916) staged a military coup against Madero and took over the government in 1913. President Woodrow Wilson called Huerta's regime "a government of butchers." The U.S. government lifted an embargo against shipping arms to Mexico in order to send guns to Venustiano Carranza (1859–1920), Huerta's opposition. Wilson also set up a barricade at Veracruz to stop nations from sending arms to Huerta's forces. Then a few American sailors assigned to Veracruz were arrested for trespassing in a restricted area. There was little fuss over the matter, and they eventually were freed. However, to extract an apology, the United States demanded that the Mexicans fire a salute to the U.S. flag. When they did not comply, Congress used the Tampico Incident, as it was called, as an excuse to send military forces into Mexico to oust Huerta. A war between the United States and Mexico was narrowly averted when both nations agreed to mediation from Argentina, Brazil, and Chile—known as "The ABC Powers." During the summer of 1914, Huerta fled Mexico and Carranza took office. In 1915, the United States recognized Carranza's government.

This caused problems with Francisco "Pancho" Villa (1877–1923), who, though once aligned with Carranza, eventually battled against Carranza's forces as a revolutionary, trying to improve life for the people of

Mexican revolutionary Francisco "Pancho" Villa tried to improve life for the Mexican people by battling Venustiano Carranza's forces.
Reproduced by permission of Archive Photos, Inc.

Mexico. Villa had waged a campaign for land reforms and attempted to set up a relationship with the U.S. government, knowing that being officially recognized by the United States was important in reaching the goals of reform and revolution he had in mind. When it became clear that the United States would instead officially recognize Carranza as Mexico's leader, Villa turned his revolutionary attention to killing Americans. In January 1916, Villa's soldiers murdered sixteen U.S. mining engineers. Two months later, he razed the town of Columbus, New Mexico, killing seventeen Americans. U.S. general John J. Pershing (1860–1948) and troops headed for Mexico to destroy Villa, but they could not locate him.

Pancho Villa was assassinated in 1923 by enemies within Mexico. He is remembered as a folk hero in Mexican popular culture. He shares that legacy with another Mexican revolutionary of the period, Emiliano Zapata (c. 1883–1919), who also called for land reforms and fought corrupt Mexican leaders of the decade.

❖ AMERICA AT WAR: FROM NEUTRALITY TO ENGAGEMENT

The Great War, or World War I as it later was known, broke out during the summer of 1914 among the five "Big Powers" of Europe: Austria-Hungary, Great Britain, France, Germany, and Russia. Political, economic, and military tensions had long existed among these nations. However, the event that sparked the war was the assassination of Austria-Hungary's Archduke Franz Ferdinand (1863–1914) by a Serbian nationalist on June 28, 1914 in Sarajevo. Subsequent diplomatic maneuvering could not stop the flood of distrust and hatred that had been building up across Europe. Much of the continent went to war: Germany, Austria-Hungary, and Italy (The Central Powers) fought against Great Britain, France, and Russia (The Allies). (Italy would later realign itself against the Central Powers.)

Battles raged across Europe for four years and four months, resulting in incalculable injuries, deaths, and mass destruction. Conservative estimates record the number of deaths at ten million and the number of maimed and injured at about twenty million. One of the reasons for the war's extended duration was the relative equality of economic, industrial, and military assets held by each country as the conflict began. The opponents were closely matched, which made for a drawn-out series of conflicts.

President Wilson resolved to keep America out of the war, but his intentions for neutrality were doomed by world events. On May 7, 1915, a German submarine torpedoed the British passenger liner *Lusitania* off the coast of Ireland as it traveled from the United States to Great Britain. The ship sank, and 1,198 people—including 128 Americans—died. Wilson protested the attack, which infuriated U.S. secretary of state William Jennings Bryan (1860–1925). Bryan felt that Wilson's actions broke with America's neutral stance, and he resigned. The Germans defended their attack on the *Lusitania* by saying they had issued warnings that they would sink all ships attempting to travel in the Atlantic zone. Furthermore, the Germans claimed that the ocean liner was carrying arms to Great Britain, which it was. Still, Germany agreed to stop unrestricted submarine warfare, and Wilson was appeased. U.S. neutrality would continue, for the moment.

In 1916, the British tightened economic restrictions on Germany by stopping shipments from entering German territory. British citizens were told to boycott eighty-seven companies in the United States that were selling goods to Germany. Despite this economic dispute, U.S. sympathies lay with the allied interests of France, Great Britain, and Russia. Germany's reengagement in unrestricted submarine warfare in the Atlantic on January 31, 1917, also reinforced the U.S. relationship with the Allies. During the first few months of 1917 the sinking of four U.S. ships resulted in fifteen American deaths. Other incidents occurred, as well, that made it clear that the United States could no longer remain detached from the conflict. Wilson called for war on April 2, 1917. Congress backed the president, and the United States formally declared war against the Central Powers on April 6 of that year.

❖ AMERICA AT WAR: THE HOMEFRONT

Now that the United States was at war, preparations had to be made to ensure victory. By tradition, little of the federal budget had been spent on military matters. From 1900 to 1914, only 1 percent of the gross national product (GNP) was spent on defense. Now, however, priorities changed. There was a need to create a powerful defense and offense by building up the arms and munitions industry. America also needed to form and train its military forces. In May 1916, concerned that U.S.-Mexican relations were deteriorating, the government had passed the National Defense Act, which authorized an army of 223,000 men and a National Guard of 450,000 members. On May 18, 1917, that act was supplemented with the Selective Service Act, calling for a wartime draft. By the war's end, U.S. war expenses would total $17.1 billion for the development of a wartime military force.

During the war, the government took on extraordinary powers in order to stabilize the country's economy and maintain the political control of those in power. Bureaus such as the War Industries Board and the War Labor Board regulated business and industry. The railroads were placed under government control through the Federal Railroad Administration. The Espionage and Sedition Acts allowed the government to monitor the activities of anyone they believed might be engaged in activities designed to undermine the political or economic stability of the United States; this led to jail time for some individuals and restrictions on speech and other forms of communication for many others. Many activities were regulated for the first time: commercial shipping was controlled by the Shipping Act of 1916, and the publication and dissemination of ideas and information was monitored and restricted by the Committee on Public Information (also known as the Creel Committee).

The Zimmermann Telegram

In early 1917 Arthur Zimmermann, the German foreign secretary, sent a top-secret message confirming unrestricted submarine warfare as of February 1, and proposing a German-Mexican alliance against the United States. The communication was sent to the German foreign minister in Mexico via the German ambassador to the United States. Fortunately for Americans, it was intercepted by the British and presented to President Woodrow Wilson. Wilson announced the contents to the American public, and before long, the United States declared war on Germany.

❖ AMERICA AT WAR: THE AMERICAN EXPEDITIONARY FORCES IN EUROPE

After four years of fighting, brutal trench warfare had weakened the military forces of all involved countries. This style of combat consisted of opposing forces shooting and otherwise attacking each other from fairly permanent trenches (ditches) protected by barbed wire. Forces from Great Britain and Italy were ravaged, and French armies had mutinied. Russia's forces had been sent to war by the czar, but revolutionary armies had toppled the royal dictator in 1917, leaving the Russian military without decisive leadership. Understandably, the U.S. declaration of war was greeted enthusiastically by the Allied forces (which were earlier known as the "Triple Entente" of France, Great Britain, and Russia). For the Allies, the American Expeditionary Forces (AEF) would provide needed reinforcement and bolster the spirits of the war-weary Allied troops. The Allies assumed that, under the command of U.S. general John J. Pershing (1860–1948), the AEF soon would turn the tide of the war. Yet it would be a year before the AEF touched European soil.

After declaring war, the United States quickly proceeded to build an expansive military force. By the spring of 1918, sixty-two divisions of twenty-eight thousand men each, a total of 3.7 million soldiers, made up the U.S. Army. Forty-two divisions sailed for Europe and began fighting on April 20, 1918. Through the spring, American soldiers fought fierce, bloody battles against the forces of Germany and its Central Powers allies (Austria-Hungary, Bulgaria, and Turkey). In early June, the U.S. Second and Third Divisions joined the Allies to stop the Germans from capturing

Paris. From June 6 to June 21, U.S. Marines fought against the Germans at Belleau Wood. More than eighteen hundred U.S. troops were killed and eight thousand other soldiers died in that brutal battle. Sixteen hundred Germans were taken prisoner.

After nearly four years of harsh battles, the Central Powers were unable to withstand the strength of the newly arrived Americans. The Central Powers waged their final offensive in July 1918, against French and American forces along the Marne River in France. On September 26, the AEF began the crucial battle known as the Meuse-Argonne offensive. The scene was hellish, demonstrating the poor preparation of the hastily trained U.S. troops. The sad result: 120,000 American casualties. During the battle, French Premier Georges Clemenceau (1841–1929) became so disturbed by Pershing's methods that he would have asked Wilson to remove the general from his command if colleagues had not intervened.

However, the resources of the Central Powers were decimated. Germany and its partners had become undone, and the war was ending. Turkey quit the war on October 30. Four days later, Austria-Hungary pulled out. On November 9, Kaiser Wilhelm II (1859–1941), the leader of Germany, escaped to the Netherlands. The factions agreed to sign an armistice (a temporary halt to hostilities by agreement between opponents) on November 11, 1918. Finally, the war was over. The United States had played a relatively brief but influential role and suffered 116,516 war deaths. Of these, 53,402 were battle deaths; 63,114 were due to other causes, mainly disease stemming from the horrible conditions on the fields and in the trenches. An additional two hundred thousand American soldiers were maimed or injured in the bloodiest war that had been fought to date.

❖ WOODROW WILSON'S PEACE PLAN

On January 8, 1919, President Woodrow Wilson addressed Congress with a list of peace terms known as the Fourteen Points. Wilson stressed that the United States would ask for neither European territory nor reparations (money paid by a defeated nation in compensation for damages caused during a war). The United States would partake in neither secrecy nor intrigue and simply wanted a just peace under a new international political system. On January 18, The Big Four—Wilson, Prime Minister David Lloyd George of Great Britain, Premier Georges Clemenceau of France, and Prime Minister Vittorio Orlando of Italy—convened at Versailles, just outside Paris. There they negotiated a peace treaty that included Wilson's concept for a League of Nations to mediate international disputes in order to avoid future wars. Unfortunately, the U.S. Congress refused to ratify the Treaty of Versailles. Because of this, the United States

British Prime Minister David Lloyd George (left), French Prime Minister Georges Clemenceau (center), and U.S. President Woodrow Wilson meeting in Versailles, France, for the 1919 peace conference.
Reproduced by permission of Archive Photos, Inc.

did not join the League of Nations when it was instituted, and Congress did not sign a formal treaty ending the war until 1921.

❖ THE RED SCARE

In 1917, while the nations of Europe were enmeshed in war, revolution was taking place in Russia. Czar Nicholas II (1868–1918) was overthrown,

The Woman's Peace Party

The Woman's Peace Party (WPP) was established in January 1915 to give "the mother half of humanity" a voice in world affairs. Jane Addams (1860–1935), a social worker who had founded Hull House in Chicago, became its first president. The party platform called for mediation to end the war in Europe, arms limitations, and the legalization of the vote for women. The WPP became known throughout the world when Addams presided at the International Congress of Women, held at The Hague, Netherlands, in April 1915. In its second year, the WPP boasted twenty-five thousand members. Once America entered World War I, the WPP began advocating a design for international peace, and in May 1919, helped establish the Women's International League for Peace and Freedom.

and a provisional government under the leadership of Aleksandr Kerensky (1881–1970) was formed. Kerensky's government was weak, and soon was displaced by the communist Bolsheviks, referred to as "Reds," led by Vladimir Lenin (1870–1924). The Reds of the newly formed Soviet Union sought to spread communism (a political and economic doctrine based upon socialism as interpreted by Karl Marx [1818–1883] and Lenin, by which property is not privately owned but controlled by the state). During the late 1910s, communists were accused of sending bombs to many U.S. government officials. Some American intellectuals and social activists, many of whom were foreign-born, were sympathetic to the communist doctrine. Those who supported communism or tried to spread the doctrine in the United States were considered dangerous radicals and threats to the American way of life. There was a media campaign against Reds, and public hysteria led to job dismissals, book bannings and burnings, and even violence. Eventually the fearful climate of the "Red Scare" subsided when Warren Harding (1865–1923) was elected president in late 1920; his campaign platform had promised a return to normalcy.

❖ FEMINISM AND WOMEN'S RIGHT TO VOTE

On June 4, 1919, Congress passed the Nineteenth Amendment, which granted women the right to vote. By August 1920, the requisite number of states had ratified the legislation. Fifty years after the passage of the Fif-

A suffragist picketing in front of the White House. Suffragists were women who picketed, marched, and demonstrated to earn the right to vote.
Reproduced by permission of the Corbis Corporation.

teenth Amendment granting all men the right to vote, women were finally accorded this right. Advocates for women's suffrage had held their first major convention at Seneca Falls, New York, in 1848. By 1910, more than seventy-five thousand members belonged to the National American Women Suffrage Association; by 1917 there were more than two million. For years, advocates had staged rallies, paraded, and even picketed the White House. Some were jailed. A few, such as militant suffragist Alice Paul (1885–1977), endured hunger strikes leading to painful force-feedings by jailers. Paul even spent a week imprisoned in a psychiatric ward because of her belief in a woman's right to vote.

❖ THE BATTLE FOR RACIAL EQUALITY

African Americans, particularly those in the South, did not share in the civil rights that were taken for granted by other U.S. citizens. By 1910, black men in the South were kept from exercising their right to vote through poll taxes (which poor blacks could not afford) and literacy tests (which less-educated blacks could not pass). They were paid less than whites in comparable jobs, and their education system was inferior. When African Americans bought tickets to mixed-race movie theaters, they had to sit in the upper balcony. Certain theaters were for whites only; others were designated for blacks. When they boarded buses, blacks could sit only in back seats. These discriminatory statutes were called "Jim Crow" laws.

During the late 1910s, more than three hundred thousand African Americans headed north to work in wartime industries. Even if most of these blacks were not welcomed into the fabric of their new communities, at least they had escaped the repressive Jim Crow laws. In May 1910, the National Association for the Advancement of Colored People (NAACP) was created to deal with such issues as education, legislation, and litigation on behalf of African Americans. In one of the NAACP's most important legal cases, *Buchanan* v. *Warley,* the Supreme Court ruled that segregated housing in Louisville, Kentucky, was unconstitutional. The NAACP and other civil liberties groups fought to put an end to the gruesome crime of lynching African Americans. Seventy-six lynchings (deaths of black men by hanging or mob beatings on the part of white men) were recorded in the United States in 1910, followed by sixty-seven in 1911. In 1919, there were eighty-three lynchings. Late in the decade, a number of large race riots broke out in major cities, ending with white courts handing down harsh sentences, including extended prison terms, to participants. A few rioters were even executed for protesting against racism.

❖ PROHIBITION AND THE EIGHTEENTH AMENDMENT

The drinking of beverages containing alcohol had long been a concern of certain Americans. By the mid-nineteenth century, thirteen states had prohibited alcoholic drinks. Despite the protests of many Americans, particularly working class males, Catholics, and German and Irish immigrants, Congress passed the Eighteenth Amendment on December 22, 1917, to extend this restriction to all states. It was ratified on January 29, 1919. The law, which ushered in a chapter of American life known as

In 1914 Congress enacted The Harrison Narcotic Act, authorizing the federal government to record narcotics transactions and restricting narcotics use to medical purposes. Americans increasingly viewed the open trade and distribution of narcotics as threatening to public morality. Prior attempts to control the sale of drugs and fraudulent medicines had failed. In New York, legislators stalled the passage of laws to prohibit the rampant use of cocaine, fearing that restrictions would adversely affect manufacturers of medicines and interfere with doctor-patient relationships. In 1919, the Supreme Court upheld the legality of the Harrison Narcotic Act and confirmed the federal government's right to regulate the dissemination of drugs.

"Prohibition," prohibited, or outlawed, the manufacture, sale, transport, import, and export of intoxicating liquor. In other words, the United States went "dry." The amendment was not repealed until 1933, by which time the unlawful production and sale of alcoholic beverages had become a major economic and political issue.

❖ NATIONAL POLITICS AND THE ELECTIONS OF 1912 TO 1918

1912

The Republican Party (also known as the Grand Old Party [GOP]) was in terrible shape when three hundred delegates walked out of the Republican National Convention to form the Progressive Party and nominated former U.S. president Theodore Roosevelt (1858–1919) as their candidate. Meanwhile, incumbent President William Howard Taft (1857–1930) held onto the Republican nomination. Although his administration had led the nation to prosperity, Taft did not have the political skills to hold his party together. He alienated key party members and backers by failing to provide adequate tariff reforms, and his tenure was tainted by scandal.

The Republican platform was conservative. Even so, it called for certain labor reforms, including workmen's compensation legislation and a limit on work hours for women and children, land reclamation, and a federal trade commission to regulate interstate commerce.

Roosevelt's Progressive platform of "New Nationalism" was one of the most reform-minded campaigns in the history of the United States. He called for consumer protection, votes for women, labor reforms for women and children, and government regulation of corporations.

Woodrow Wilson, a relative newcomer to national politics, won the Democratic Party nomination. His "New Freedom" campaign embraced a Jeffersonian model of federal government wherein power should be used to eliminate privilege, remove roadblocks to individual initiative, and restore and preserve a climate of competition in business. A former "trustbuster," Roosevelt believed in 1912 that corporate trusts (combinations of companies run by a powerful few that discouraged competition in the marketplace) could be regulated, but Wilson insisted that they be "busted."

It was a rough campaign. On October 14, before giving a speech in Milwaukee, Roosevelt suffered a gunshot wound during an attempted assassination. He delivered his speech, however, before being taken to hospital for treatment. By the end of the campaign, Wilson won the presidency with 435 electoral votes. Roosevelt collected 88, and the incumbent Taft secured just 8 electoral votes. Democrats also controlled both the Senate and the House of Representatives.

1916

In June 1916, Republican Party representatives gathered for their national convention in Chicago. They conceived a moderately progressive campaign platform, called for a protective tariff, and attacked Wilson's foreign policy. They favored child labor laws, a rural credit system, and workmen's compensation legislation for federal employees. The delegates nominated Supreme Court Justice Charles Evans Hughes (1862–1948) as the Republican presidential nominee.

Republicans were optimistic about the race. They felt that Wilson's election in 1912 was due only to a split in the Republican Party, a weakness they avoided in 1916. The Progressive Party had invited Theodore Roosevelt to be their candidate again, but he declined. As a result, there was ultimately no Progressive candidate in the race. Since the 1914 elections had brought a number of Republicans into Congressional seats, the Republicans were feeling upbeat.

Several days after the Republicans convened, the Democratic Convention gathered in St. Louis, Missouri. The incumbent, Wilson, would be the party's nominee. However, instead of running on the "New Freedom" platform, Wilson presented a series of issues built around "Americanism." He called for more government regulation of child labor, wages, and workmen's compensation for federal employees. The Democratic ideal held to isolationism; one slogan of Wilson supporters was: "He kept us out of war." Still, Wilson's speeches began to express a bent towards internationalism. He declared that the United States should strive "to use its power…to make secure its just interests throughout the world…and…to assist the world in securing settled peace and justice."

Wilson's moderately progressive campaign helped to move the Democratic Party away from the conservatism of past years, starting a trend that would become more pronounced under the leadership of Franklin Delano Roosevelt (1882–1945) in the 1930s. During the campaign, Republican Hughes argued against Wilson's views on the economy and foreign policy. He stressed the need to expand America's preparedness program. Hughes called for "America first, America efficient." Additionally, he faulted Wilson's dealings with Mexico and his inability to control Atlantic Ocean travel and trade rights in the face of German aggression.

Wilson won the election with 277 electoral votes, just 23 more than Hughes collected. In Congressional elections, the Democrats lost 3 seats in the Senate but maintained a majority of 53 to 42. They also kept a narrow margin in the House, winning 216 seats to 210 Republican seats and 6 seats for minority party members.

1918

The 1918 elections were held at a pivotal time in America's history. Just days before the signing of the armistice to end World War I, and during one of the worst flu epidemics in American history, the Republican Party regained strength and retook majorities in the House and Senate. This upheaval meant that Wilson no longer could rely on congressional support to enact his policies.

❖ LEGISLATING CHILD LABOR

In 1910, there were an estimated two million children working in industrial settings in the United States. Prior to the 1910s, child labor had been evident in the workplace. Farms, small mills, and retail stores regularly hired children as a cheap source of labor. While the rise of modern industrialism in the United States did not bring about child labor, it made the issue more pronounced. During the first years of the twentieth century, reformers such as Jacob Riis, George Creel, and Denver Judge Ben Lindsey made the public aware of the wretched conditions under which children toiled in the canning industry, the glass industry (where young boys molded glass objects near blistering hot furnaces for hours on end), anthracite mining (where boys sorted mined coal by hand), and the sweatshops of the textile industry. As machinery became larger and more motorized, children grew increasingly susceptible to maimings. Furthermore, as society began to acknowledge the importance of education to create productive citizens, reformers made an effective case that children who worked ten-hour shifts were provided no opportunity for schooling.

In 1911, the U.S. Commission on Uniform Laws was urged to adopt a uniform child labor law to establish minimum standards for youngsters working under hazardous health conditions. In 1912, a special bureau was set up within the Department of Labor to handle the regulation of child labor. These gestures were ineffective, particularly due to disparities among state laws. In mid-decade, Wilson influenced Congress to enact The Owen-Keating Bill, which restricted shipments of goods produced through child labor, but the Supreme Court ruled the bill unconstitutional. The Court based its ruling on the belief that Congress, under the Tenth Amendment, had no authority to control conditions of production in individual states. Despite this setback, public support continued to rise against child labor and further legislation would be launched against its evils.

A child worker in a mine in West Virginia. Child laborers often had to work in factories, mines, and other environments that were hazardous and depressing.

❖ WORKERS' COMPENSATION

Between 1910 and 1919, the policy of employers changed regarding compensation of workers injured while on the job. At the decade's start, each worker was responsible for personal injuries. The only way a worker could collect damages for losses was to sue the employer. During the first decade of the century, close to thirty-five thousand deaths per year occurred as a result of workplace incidents. By 1911, as momentum among businesses increased towards compensating disabled workers, the National Association of Manufacturers (NAM) encouraged the adoption of a system of workers' compensation that would dispense with expensive, time-consuming litigation. Employers were asked to help design new policies, and were directed to purchase insurance policies against accidents. Compensation would be based on predetermined schedules. Claims would be evaluated by an administrative agency.

Industries began introducing safety measures into the workplace. In 1911 and 1913, Congress required the railroad industry to implement the

In 1912, the U.S. Bureau of Labor surveyed 296 state prisons where eighty-six thousand men and women were confined. Of those inmates, fifty-one thousand were employed by private contractors and industry. Almost all prison laborers were paid wages far below free laborers, and they were in danger of severe punishments if they failed to perform well. In corrupt prisons, inmates worked under slave conditions. They were deprived of sufficient food, and their wages were distributed to those who ran the prisons. Although voices spoke in opposition, the practice of convict labor would continue until the beginning of World War II (1941–45).

use of safety equipment. Similarly, improvements in factory and mining environments began to be instituted. By 1917, the Supreme Court upheld workers' compensation laws that had recently passed in New York. In 1919, the Court upheld similar legislation in Arizona.

❖ THE MANN ACT

During the first years of the century, ghastly tales were publicized about the abduction of innocent young women for the purpose of prostitution. Stories of immigrant girls, in particular, who were made to work in brothels in large cities across the nation spurred reformers to push for protective legislation against what was known as white slave trafficking. This practice was prohibited under The Mann Act of 1910. Section Two of The Mann Act stipulates that anyone who knowingly transports a young woman across state lines for the purpose of "prostitution or debauchery" is guilty of a felony. The Supreme Court upheld the statute.

For More Information

BOOKS

Altman, Linda Jacobs. *The Decade that Roared: America During Prohibition.* New York: Twenty-First Century Books, 1997.

Bartoletti, Susan Campbell. *Growing Up in Coal Country.* Boston: Houghton Mifflin Juvenile, 1996.

Brown, Gene. *Conflict in Europe and the Great Depression: World War I.* New York: Twenty-First Century Books, 1993.

Cooper, Michael L. *Hell Fighters: African American Soldiers in World War I.* New York: Lodestar Books, 1997.

Dolan, Edward F. *America in World War I.* Brookfield, CT: Millbrook Press, 1996.

Gawne, Jonathan. *Over There!: The American Soldier in World War I.* Philadelphia, Chelsea House.

Gourley, Catherine. *Good Girl Work: Sweatshops, and How Women Changed Their Role in the American Workforce.* Brookfield, CT: Millbrook Press, 1999.

Hatt, Christine. *World War I, 1914–1918.* New York: Franklin Watts, 2001.

Kent, Zachary. *World War I: The War to End All Wars.* Hillside, NJ: Enslow Publishers, 1994.

Lucas, Eileen. *The Eighteenth and Twenty-First Amendments: Alcohol—Prohibition and Repeal.* Springfield, NJ: Enslow Publishers, 1998.

Randolph, Sallie G. *Woodrow Wilson.* New York: Walker & Company, 1992.

Rogers, James T. *Woodrow Wilson: Visionary for Peace.* New York: Facts on File, 1997.

Sommerville, Donald. *World War I.* Austin, TX: Raintree/Steck Vaughn, 1997.

Uschan, Michael V. *A Multicultural Portrait of World War I.* Tarrytown, NY: Benchmark Books, 1996.

WEB SITES

American Cultural History: The Twentieth Century, 1910–1919. http://www.nhm-ccd.cc.tx.us/contracts/lrc/kc/decade10.html (accessed on August 2, 2002).

Children at Work, 1908–1912. http://www.ibiscom.com/hnintro.htm (accessed on August 2, 2002).

Colonel Edward House 1858–1938. http://www.pbs.org/wgbh/amex/wilson/peopleevents/p_house.html (accessed on August 2, 2002).

U.S. National Archives and Records Administration. The Constitution: The 19th Amendment. http://www.archives.gov/exhibit_hall/charters_of_freedom/constitution/19th_amendment.html (accessed on August 2, 2002).

The White House. Woodrow Wilson. http://www.whitehouse.gov/history/presidents/ww28.html (accessed on August 2, 2002).

chapter five *Lifestyles and Social Trends*

1910: Levi Strauss and Company begins making children's clothes, the first major line of casual play clothing for youngsters.

1910: Architect Frank Lloyd Wright begins construction on Taliesin, his new studio and house in rural Wisconsin.

1910: **February 6** Chicago publisher William Dickson Boyce founds the Boy Scouts of America.

1910: **May 1** The National Negro Committee becomes known as the National Association for the Advancement of Colored People (NAACP).

1910: **July** The South-American style ballroom dance called the tango increases in popularity among New York City couples.

1910: **September 18–25** The National Conference of Catholic Charities holds its first meeting at the Catholic University of America. The members coordinate the nationwide efforts of lay and diocesan social work agencies.

1911: The fabric rayon, called "artificial silk," is introduced by the American Viscose Company.

1911: **March 25** A fire at the Triangle Shirtwaist Factory on New York City's Lower East Side results in the death of 146 female workers.

1911: **May 7** Three thousand women march down Fifth Avenue in New York City, demanding the right to vote.

1912: The dance team of Irene and Vernon Castle popularize ballroom dancing. Furthermore, Irene's lightweight, unrestricted clothing serves as a model for women to adopt more comfortable fashions.

1912: An African American preacher of mysterious background called Father Divine, whose birth name is George Baker, begins his first preaching mission in Americus, Georgia. His followers would come to view him as the Second Coming of Jesus Christ.

1912: **April 15** The luxury ship *Titanic* sinks on its maiden voyage, killing 1,517 passengers and crew.

1912: **May 1** The elegant Beverly Hills Hotel is constructed on what once had been a California bean field.

1913: Midway Gardens, an amusement park and concert hall designed by Frank Lloyd Wright, opens in Chicago.

1913: The Jewish Anti-Defamation League is established.

1914: "Coco" Chanel opens her first dress shop in France.

1914: **May 7** Congress passes a resolution to celebrate Mother's Day on the second Sunday in May.

1914: **November** Mary Phelps Jacob, later known as Caresse Crosby, patents her design for the first brassiere (a woman's undergarment with cups to support the bust).

1915: The Victor Talking Machine company introduces a record player called the Victrola.

1916: Automobile and truck production in the United States passes 1 million new vehicles per year. There are more than 3.5 million cars on the road.

1916: **Summer** The distinctive hoop-skirt-shaped Coca-Cola bottle is first manufactured at the Root Glass Company in Terre Haute, Indiana.

1916: **October 16** The first birth control clinic for poor and immigrant women opens in Brooklyn, New York, through the efforts of Margaret Sanger.

1917: **May 18** The Selective Service Act passes, which authorizes federal conscription (required enrollment in military service) and requires U.S. male citizens aged twenty-one to thirty to register for enrollment.

1918: For one of the few times in American history, the U.S. population decreases. The decline of fifty thousand is blamed on World War I (1914–18) casualties, postponed marriages, fewer immigrations, and a devastating epidemic of influenza (flu).

1918: A toy company in New York City starts manufacturing Raggedy Ann dolls. Soon the production grows into a $20-million-per-year business.

1919: Architect Julia Morgan begins to oversee the construction of San Simeon, the huge, ultra-luxurious mansion of publisher William Randolph Hearst. It is located one hundred miles north of Santa Barbara, California.

1919: **July 20** Roaming bands of soldiers, sailors, and Marines attack African Americans on the streets of Washington, D.C., claiming blacks have been attacking white women.

1919: **July and August** Race riots in Chicago and Washington, D.C., as well as in several Southern and Midwestern states, result in the deaths of hundreds of people.

Overview

During the 1910s, new developments in government, big business, and industry began to change daily life in the United States. America was becoming an urban, industrial nation as the younger population increasingly left farms to settle in big cities. As they moved into closer proximity to each other and made increasing amounts of disposable income, people were becoming more fashion and lifestyle conscious.

Lifestyles became more active and fashions became more functional. Clothing that restricted movement and distorted the look of the body became outdated. Meanwhile, the rise of national magazines helped spread an interest in fashions and trends, making a single style accessible to people of varied economic classes. Automobiles began to take on a stylish look. While there were no general changes in the Ford Model T, the era's top-selling car, other manufacturers produced cars that catered to more affluent customers. Through technical advances, these cars became more efficient to make and operate. Plus, they no longer resembled old-fashioned carriages.

Buildings, too, sported modern architectural designs. While many skyscrapers, government buildings, and monuments were designed in the style of the Beaux Arts school, which used older European decorative styles, smaller commercial structures and many private homes were designed in a sleek, functional manner to reflect new lifestyle trends.

There also were new jobs available to women outside the home. As women began earning wages, they started to be strong, active consumers. For that reason, manufacturers began producing fashionable clothing and household devices specifically for females. Still, for most of the decade, women did not have the right to vote. Suffragists (those who advocated granting women the right to vote) marched on and even picketed the White House until equal voting rights for women were adopted.

Throughout the decade, several segments of society continued to be outsiders. Most African Americans approached the coming of World War I (1914–18) with courage and patriotism, but they continued to be treated as inferiors by white America. Certain immigrant groups also were isolated and viewed with distrust by the mainstream. As the war in Europe escalated, German Americans were viewed as enemies because the Germans were the enemy in Europe. Many European immigrants actually returned to their homelands before the outbreak of war could cut all ties with loved ones. Immigrants who remained in the United States were urged to assimilate (become absorbed into the American mainstream).

In the realm of religion, a missionary spirit enveloped much of America as religious leaders spread various doctrines of Christianity to people across the country. Also, evangelists such as Billy Sunday preached fiery messages about sin, mortality, and the righteousness of America's participation in the war.

Marcus Garvey (1887–1940) British West Indies activist and black nationalist Marcus Garvey moved to Harlem in 1916, where his philosophies had a tremendous impact on the African American community. Through his newspaper the *Negro World*, established in 1918, he preached the importance of unity for the black race and called for a return to the African homeland. In 1919, Garvey bought a ship and sold tickets for his "Back to Africa" movement. Soon he controlled three ships called the Black Star Line and actually headed six voyages to Africa. However, the Black Star Line was mismanaged, and Garvey was convicted of mail fraud. He spent two years in prison and then was deported to Jamaica.

Cass Gilbert (1859–1934) Cass Gilbert was the architect for the Woolworth Building (1913) in New York City. He adorned this early skyscraper with Gothic-style, terra cotta gargoyles (grotesque, carved animal or human figures), and, at 792 feet, it remained the world's tallest building until 1930. A leading Beaux-Arts architect of the early twentieth century, Gilbert designed such prominent public buildings as the St. Louis (Missouri) Central Public Library (1912), the Detroit (Michigan) Public Library (1914), and in Washington, D.C., the U.S. Treasury Annex (1919), and the U.S. Supreme Court Building (1935). He served as president of the American Institute of Architects from 1908 to 1909, and as a member the National Commission of Fine Arts from 1910 to 1918. *Photo reproduced by permission of the Corbis Corporation.*

Joe Hill (1879–1915) Swedish immigrant Joe Hill was a laborer and songwriter. Between 1902 and 1910, he traveled through the United States taking odd jobs, and in 1910 he joined the Industrial Workers of the World (IWW), a union of socialists advocating violent upheaval of the capitalist system. Hill's songs, particularly "The Preacher and the Slave," glorified the workers' struggle, raising morale among his fellow Wobblies (IWW members). In July 1914, Hill was convicted on a dubious murder charge and executed by a firing squad in November 1915. Many rallied around Hill as a victim of the capitalist system. He is immortalized in dramatic works and song as a working class hero and legend. *Photo reproduced by permission of the Corbis Corporation.*

John R. Mott (1865–1955) The life goal of John R. Mott was to spread the gospel of Christianity, and he became America's greatest organizer of missionaries. His work intensified as war broke out in 1914, and he tried to spread ideas of peace to the warring nations. From 1915 to 1928, he served as general secretary of the Young Men's Christian Association (YMCA). He was also chairman of the Student Volunteer Movement for Foreign Missions (SVMFM), dedicated to the "evangelization of the world in this generation." Because Mott's missionary work was so important to him, he turned down a number of prestigious positions, including U.S. ambassador to China, president of Princeton University, and dean of the Yale Divinity School. *Photo courtesy of the Library of Congress.*

Alice Paul (1885–1977) Suffragist Alice Paul grew up among Quakers, a religious group who advocated voting rights for women. She obtained a Ph.D. in social work from the University of Pennsylvania in 1912, and set out for Washington, D.C., to lobby Congress and President Wilson to pass a federal amendment granting women the right to vote. After years of effort—which included lobbying, educating, picketing, and even going to jail for five weeks—she succeeded in convincing Congress to enact the Nineteenth Amendment in 1919, which gave women the right to vote. She then returned to school and earned three law degrees. For the remainder of her long life, Paul lobbied for the passage of an Equal Rights Amendment to assure equality for women in all aspects of American life. *Photo reproduced by permission of the Corbis Corporation.*

George Santayana (1863–1952) From 1889 to 1912, Spanish American George Santayana was a professor of philosophy at Harvard University. One of America's most influential philosophers, Santayana's message of Ethical Idealism stressed the importance of testing truth through experience; to his way of thinking, beliefs should be based on evidence, rather than blind faith. Young intellectuals who were questioning the foundations of industrial capitalism sought guidance through Santayana's writings. His most renowned writings include *The Sense of Beauty* (1896), *The Life of Reason, or the Phases of Human Progress* (1906–17; five volumes), *Scepticism and Animal Faith* (1922), and *Realms of Being* (1927–40; four volumes). *Photo reproduced courtesy of Library of Congress.*

Topics in the News ·

❖ AFRICAN AMERICANS ENCOUNTER RACISM DURING WORLD WAR I

During the 1910s, African Americans were plagued by racial prejudice. At the time, 90 percent of blacks lived in areas such as the South where Jim Crow laws (a system of laws that kept black people separated from whites) segregated them in every aspect of daily life. Schools, restaurants, and theaters were designated for "whites only" and "blacks only," as were drinking fountains and restrooms. Because the administration of President Woodrow Wilson (1856–1924) was comprised of men of influence who favored racial segregation, policies of racism extended into the various federal departments. For example, as the United States entered World War I in 1917, the U.S. Armed Forces, under Secretary of War Newton D. Baker (1871–1937), increased its manpower and became one of America's most racially divided institutions.

The majority of African Americans were very supportive of the war effort, purchasing Liberty Bonds (investments that helped finance the military), working on drives to conserve materials needed for the war effort, and serving on draft boards. Many imagined that their patriotic efforts would lead to a more balanced image of blacks as good citizens. This, however, was not to be. Of the 5,300 blacks who joined the U.S. Navy, most were restricted to servant positions. The Marines accepted no blacks. The army drafted many African American professionals such as doctors and dentists; however, instead of becoming commissioned officers, they were given the lowly rank of private. Few African Americans were given positions considered prestigious and responsible. Black soldiers lived and trained separately. Their morale was low, and so they sometimes failed to fight well at the front lines. The 369th Infantry from New York, however, performed courageously on the front lines, and was honored by the French government for its bravery.

❖ AMERICANS EXPRESS ANTIWAR SENTIMENTS

When Congress declared war in April 1917, public reaction was divided for reasons of ethnicity, national allegiance, and philosophy. Russian American Jews resented being allied with Russia, having experienced persecution from that nation's established order. Austro-Hungarian Americans and German Americans bristled at depictions of their homelands as the enemy. Those who opposed the war found themselves harassed. For example, a Rutgers University student who refused to take part in a Liber-

From 1910 to 1915, a twelve-volume set of books called *The Fundamentals: A Testimony to the Truth* was published and distributed at no cost to any interested person. The books were available through the Young Men's (and Young Women's) Christian Association (YMCA and YWCA), pastors, evangelists, and missionaries. Edited by Amzi Dixon (1854–1925), a Chicago pastor, the books were commissioned and paid for, at a cost of $250,000, by oil magnate Lyman Stewart (1840–1923) and his brother Milton.

The purpose of *The Fundamentals* was to set down the truth of traditional Protestant Christianity as revealed in the Bible. The books were intended to counter the approaches of rising liberal movements that tended to compare and contrast religious texts with scientific theories such as Darwinian evolutionism, which dealt with the origin of life and the survival of the fittest.

The articles in Dixon's volumes were written by leading scholars of the conservative religious movement. They consisted of personal testimonies of religious experiences and attacked a number of non-Protestant religions and sects. The writings defended the "pure truth" of the scriptures and did not deal with political and ethical questions. While more than three million copies were distributed, the concept of Fundamentalism in religion did not develop strongly until 1918.

ty Bond rally (a get-together to promote the sale of government bonds to support the war effort) was smeared with tar and covered with feathers and then paraded through the streets of New Brunswick, New Jersey, as punishment for his antiwar political stance.

Certain members of the Socialist Party who opposed America's entry into the war were treated harshly by members of the public who backed the fight in Europe. The situation became so extreme that, in Illinois, a German American socialist who had never spoken out against the war was lynched. Members of the socialist Industrial Workers of the World (IWW) labor union were not only against America's entry into war, but also were stirring up hostilities against such American institutions as the Protestant church. In 1914, IWW members (who were known as Wobblies) went from church to church in New York City demanding overnight accommodations. "If you put us out, the floor of this place will run with blood," declared IWW leader Frank Tannenbaum (1893–1969) to one pastor. The IWW accused organized religion and popular evangelists such as Billy Sunday (1862–1935) of being hypocrites. They claimed that leaders of organized religion withheld charity. As a result, socialist labor movement members such as Joe Hill, William "Big Bill" Haywood, Morris Hillquit, John Reed, and Emma Goldman were viewed with suspicion by the government as well as by the public, and they were criticized for speaking out against the war.

Conscientious objectors (those who refused to fight based on religious convictions) were tucked away in camps. They were taunted until some gave in to being drafted into the military. Meanwhile, the American Protective League (APL), an organization of volunteers under the Justice Department, conducted loyalty investigations. They posed as federal agents, using false "Secret Service Division" cards; they employed covert tactics such as wiretapping and actually broke into the homes of people suspected of avoiding the draft. In the Slackers Raid of September 3 to 6, 1918, APL agents rounded up fifty thousand suspected draft dodgers in New York City. Even though illegal means were used to gather evidence, sixteen thousand people were found guilty of having violated the Selective Service Act.

❖ IMMIGRATION WAS A TWO-WAY STREET

Immigration patterns through the 1910s show a two-way trend. One-third of immigrants from Italy, Hungary, and Croatia who arrived between 1908 and 1914 returned to Europe. When war erupted in the "old country" in 1914, many newly arrived immigrants felt it would be in their best interests to return to their homelands before all connections were severed. At the same time, many Europeans were fleeing their homelands to avoid becoming battle casualties. The most stable group of immigrants were the Eastern European Jews, who usually stayed in the United States rather than return to their European homes where pogroms (the organized massacre of people for religious reasons) were rampant.

By 1910, more than 75 percent of the populations of New York City, Boston, Chicago, Cleveland, and Detroit were made up of immigrants and their children. Asians from China and Japan settled in San Francisco. Slavs found work in the Chicago cattle slaughterhouses or in mines in the upper Midwest. Many Italians entered the construction industry in New York City and built the subways and bridges linking the New York City boroughs. The majority of Jewish males who entered the United States between 1899 and 1914 were classified as skilled workers and found employment in New York City's garment industry as garment cutters, tailors, accountants, and even factory owners. For many immigrants, becom-

Year	Number of Immigrants	Total U.S. Population
1910	1,041,570	92,407,000
1911	878,587	93,863,000
1912	838,172	95,335,000
1913	1,197,892	97,225,000
1914	1,218,480	99,111,000
1915	326,700	100,546,000
1916	298,826	101,961,000
1917	295,403	103,268,000
1918	110,618	103,208,000
1919	141,132	104,514,000

ing American meant changing their appearances: shaving beards, cutting their hair in American styles, and adopting new fashions. They learned English; often the children learned the language in public schools and taught it to their parents. Adult schools were established by social reformers such as Jane Addams (1860–1935) and Frances Kellor (1873–1952) to help immigrant families adapt to American lifestyles.

By 1917, anti-German feelings mushroomed into a kind of hysteria among Americans, who were coming to view all immigrants as potential enemies. As stories of German atrocities in Europe, such as the rape and murder of women and children, filled magazines and movie screens, this general distrust of Europeans developed into broad misgivings about the nation's immigration policies. In his third annual message to Congress, President Wilson echoed these sentiments by declaring, "There are citizens of the United States, I blush to admit, born under other flags but welcomed under our generous naturalization laws to the full freedom and opportunity of America, who have poured the poison of disloyalty in to the very arteries of our national life…. Such creatures of passion, disloyalty, and anarchy must be crushed out." In 1917, the first legislation to limit immigration was passed, requiring literacy tests for immigrants and banning many Asian laborers. Such feelings did not fade after the war ended in 1918. Three years later, Congress passed legislation to impose major restrictions on European immigration, limiting the number of Southern and Eastern Europeans who could enter the United States each year.

❖ ARCHITECTURAL STYLES LOOK BACKWARD AND TOWARD THE FUTURE

Since the 1870s, two significantly different schools of architecture had coexisted in relative harmony within U.S. cities. One school, which incorporated older styles with intricate sculpture designs, was based on the teachings of the École des Beaux Arts (the School of Fine Arts) in Paris. Additionally, this school spearheaded a revived interest in Gothic art and architecture, which had flourished in Europe from the twelfth through fifteenth centuries. The other, more modern school of architecture took its lead from the Chicago school of urban architecture and other movements that stressed simple lines and functional styling.

While the 1910s did not inaugurate any major new style of architecture, it was a time for improvements in building styles. For instance, in New York City, tall structures had become a popular design for commercial buildings. Captains of industry considered the height of their office buildings as measures of corporate success. As these skyscrapers were constructed, one next to another, they blocked the sun and even changed weather patterns on the ground level. In 1916, legislation was passed in New York City that required buildings higher than one hundred feet to be tapered away from the street. The new law resulted in better air movement and an increase in sunlight at street level. No longer would buildings be designed along the stiff, block styling of the neo-Gothic Woolworth Building (1913), designed by architect Cass Gilbert (1859–1934). In future decades, this improvement would result in skyscrapers with graceful designs, such as the Chrysler Building (1930) and the Empire State Building (1930–31). Many of the nation's grandest railroad stations were built during the 1910s. In New York City, Pennsylvania Station was completed in 1910, and Grand Central Station was opened in 1913. Both were done in the Beaux Arts fashion.

Most business structures built during the decade were examples of the Beaux Arts school, even though prominent architects such as Chicago-based Louis Sullivan (1856–1924) and his most renowned student, Frank Lloyd Wright (1867–1959), advocated the use of less-cluttered designs. Sullivan and Wright believed that "form follows function," which meant that the building's design should serve its purpose. During the decade, Sullivan designed bank buildings in the Midwest, and Wright fulfilled many contracts for his "prairie houses": structures that were long, low, and horizontal, and that mirrored the lines of the flat, open prairie. They were constructed using such natural materials as wood and stone. Wright also designed apartment houses, pavilions, gardens, hotels, and country clubs in the United States and in Japan.

Most of the major commercial and government buildings were built in the Beaux Arts style because of the conservative nature of those in charge of choosing architecture firms. It was not until 1922, when leading Finnish architect Eliel Saarinen (1873–1950) won a prize for his semi-modern design for the Chicago Tribune Building, that America's taste makers, the prominent designers and corporate and government leaders, began moving away from the Beaux-Arts school toward the simpler lines of the sleek, functional modern skyscraper.

Throughout the decade, German-born industrial designer Albert Kahn (1869–1942) designed industrial plants. His facilities had simple modern lines and plenty of windows to make maximum use of natural light. From 1909 to 1914 in Highland Park, Michigan, Kahn designed and built structures made of reinforced concrete, a relatively new building material. The plants featured large, steel-framed windows, and were designed so that all the assembly line work of building a Model T Ford could be done under one roof. In 1917, Kahn completed the half-mile-long "Building B" for the Rouge River plant near Detroit, Michigan. He continued building modern plants for Ford into the next decade.

❖ A SIMPLIFIED, CHEERFUL ENVIRONMENT IN HOME INTERIOR DESIGN

For decades, American homes had featured large, overstuffed furniture in relatively small, darkened rooms. By 1910, this style of interior home design was being condemned in magazines and homemaker manuals as old-fashioned and tasteless. The new fashion called for airy living spaces. Much of the change in taste was due to the enthusiastic acceptance of architect Frank Lloyd Wright's home plan, which featured living spaces set up to accommodate multiple activities. Older, more traditional homes for families of comfortable financial means had a separate room for each family activity: a family room for spending time with loved ones; a sitting room or parlor for visits with guests; a library for keeping books and office records; and music and sewing rooms for those activities. In the modern homes of the 1910s, the living room fulfilled the combined functions of all these old-fashioned rooms. In the spirit of combined usage, the kitchen even doubled as an informal dining room.

The colors of old-fashioned interiors had been rather dull. Walls were covered with heavily patterned wallpaper, and the furniture was uphol-

A Woman's Work Is Never Done!

As more jobs became available to women during the decade, fewer females accepted work as domestics (servants), and more housewives took paid positions outside the home. New homes were built without back staircases, since they were no longer necessary to keep house servants out of sight while they performed their duties. This modern lifestyle resulted in working women, with less time at home to do housework, having to do all the household tasks without the aid of servants.

Salvation came in a stream of newly invented, time-saving devices. Large iceboxes kept foods cold, so that they would not spoil. Gas ranges made cooking cleaner and more efficient than the old-fashioned coal-burning stoves. Hand-cranked washing machines replaced the drudgery of scrubbing laundry in tubs on finger-blistering washboards. Hot-water heaters and telephones added luxury to the middle-class lifestyle.

More than any other improvement, electricity added quality to home life. By 1919, 41 percent of Americans were using electricity to power appliances and bring a form of daylight to the home long after night had fallen.

stered in dark tones. The new interiors, however, were painted in bold colors with dark wood-stained trim. In order to take advantage of natural lighting, window trims were lightweight, without the traditional heavy layers of draperies. Shelves for books, knick-knacks, and cutlery were built into the walls.

Mission-style furniture became the most popular modern style. It was based on the Arts and Crafts Movement, a turn-of-the-century trend that originated in England and called for the use of natural elements such as wood and stone for a plain, hand-carved look. The furniture was factory-manufactured and called to mind the interior design of the Spanish missions of old California and the American Southwest. Among the most prominent makers of these pieces were Gustav Stickley (1857–1942) and his brothers, whose designs were widely copied by furniture factories across the country. Mission furniture often is made from oak and has vertical slats. It includes chairs, tables, desks, and headboards for beds. Because the chairs are not stuffed and upholstered, throw pillows often are utilized for comfort and a touch of color.

While working-class families saved to acquire a modern home with mission style interior design, the upper classes were more intrigued by the Art Nouveau style. This decor featured aspects of the human form and nature (such as trees and flowers) and was available in furniture, lamps, textiles, metalworks, clocks, and decorative glass pieces. The leading American artist and designer of Art Nouveau items was Louis Comfort Tiffany (1848–1933).

❖ AUTOMOBILE MANUFACTURERS COMPETE THROUGH STYLING AND INNOVATIONS

As the decade unfolded, the Model T automobile, manufactured by the Ford Motor Company, may not have been every American's car of choice; however, it was the only automobile that many Americans could afford. By 1914, due to the efficiency of the Ford factory assembly line process, a brand new Model T, known as a "Tin Lizzie," was turned out every twenty-four seconds! The retail cost was $440, about half of its 1908 market price of $850. With the standardization of this model, available "in any color as long as it is black," plus the availability of standard auto parts, working-class Americans were content to "have wheels." The working class did not question the color of the Model T because they did not equate automobiles with fashion.

During the 1910s, however, a number of automobile manufacturers in the United States began competing for business among customers who *could* afford a car more stylish than the Model T. These manufacturers attracted customers by offering technical innovations and design improvements. One innovative U.S. automaker was Cadillac, which in early 1911 offered an improved starter designed by Charles F. Kettering (1876–1958). In the next three years, 90 percent of American auto manufacturers also offered this starter. Only Ford, not wishing to raise its prices, did not license the starter. In 1914, two of Ford's employees, John (1864–1920) and Horace (1868–1920) Dodge, formed their own company and manufactured an all-steel-bodied car for a price just above that of the Tin Lizzie.

With the growing number of automobile manufacturing companies during the decade, more cars became available at fairly low prices. To compete for customers, carmakers paid attention to the appearance of their products as well as to the general ease of driving. In 1909, car manufacturers began to look for ways to "streamline" (give an uninterrupted flow or contour to the auto body) their models. At the fourteenth annual automobile show in New York City in 1914, there appeared a line-up of good-looking models featuring machine-pressed steel bodies. As machine pressing replaced the hand-pounding of metal sheets, automobiles proved that

A Ford Motor Company
advertisement for the
Model T, which was
efficiently built and
inexpensive to make and
purchase. *Reproduced by
permission of the Corbis
Corporation.*

they could be good looking as well as affordable. No longer did the automobile look like a nineteenth-century carriage. Even so, it would be almost twenty years until models would be sleek and really fluid in their design.

❖ FASHION FOR WOMEN REFLECTS A CHANGING LIFESTYLE

As the decade opened, women who worked for pay worked mainly in their own homes as seamstresses, laundresses, and in other peoples' homes as domestics (servants). During the decade, women increasingly took jobs in offices as typists, secretaries, and receptionists, where they were required to wear conservative, functional fashions. The old-style delicate and frilly dresses would have been intrusive and impractical in the modern office of the 1910s. When the country entered World War I in 1917, women also filled jobs that had been vacated by men who joined the military. During the war, 2.4 million women were employed in war-related industries, working in offices and on assembly lines. A functional style of clothing was needed to meet the needs of the female industrial worker.

Aside from becoming more active in the workplace, women also were learning to drive cars, enjoy ballroom dancing, and participate in sports and leisure activities. All these activities called for more comfortable clothing styles. Dresses that limited body movement also limited fun and adventure. Women said farewell to outfits that were long enough to sweep the street, weighed ten pounds, and featured awkward accessories such as deep pleats, ribbons, large adornments, and bustles (pads or frames that expanded the fullness at the back of the skirt). Modern clothing was simple and lightweight and followed the line of the body.

More than ever, clothing styles for working-class, middle-class, and even wealthy women were similar in style, due to the new widespread distribution of national magazines that featured fashions. Women of varied economic brackets had access to magazines such as *Ladies' Home Journal, Vogue,* and *Harper's Bazaar,* that showed the latest fashions. Furthermore, women no longer had to sew their family's clothing. Instead, they mail-ordered from catalogs or shopped in ready-to-wear stores, chain stores, and department stores for fashions seen in magazines. As fashion awareness spread, the difference between a typist's clothing and that of a Rockefeller or Vanderbilt was not the general look of the garment but the more subtle details of styling and fabric. Lower-priced items were mass-produced and made of standard cotton or wool. A more expensive item was custom-tailored of silk, linen, or a fine woolen gabardine or tweed. Either way, the styles were essentially the same.

Women found that skirts worn with shirtwaist blouses were a relaxed and inexpensive alternative to restrictive dresses with stiff, high-cut col-

Irene Castle, Fashion Trendsetter

Entertainer Irene Castle (1893–1969) was not only a popular ballroom dancer but also a trendsetter in women's fashion. With her husband Vernon (1887–1917), she introduced such dances as "the one-step" and "the Castle walk." In addition to her dancing, women were captivated by Castle's clothing and hairdos.

The Irene Castle "look" consisted of chiffon evening dresses that flowed in simple lines to allow for her dance performance. Castle was among the first women to abandon corsets and stiff petticoats that restricted movement and distorted the natural figure. Instead, she favored bloomers (loose underpants) and slips. When she had her hair cut to the nape of her neck and then placed a necklace on her head to keep her hair in place, women began to imitate the look.

lars. Tucked into a skirt, the blouse looked businesslike. Untucked, as became fashionable in 1914, it was suitable for leisure. By the early years of the decade, clothing manufacturers were turning out affordable fashions for middle-class women. An example is the "tailor-made," which actually was a ready-to-wear suit that cost $10 to $20. By 1910, the shirt-waist was the mainstay of many clothing manufacturers.

To meet the demand and keep prices affordable, much of this modern clothing was produced in sweatshops (factories in which workers toil for long hours at low wages under poor and sometimes hazardous conditions). Sweatshops have long been associated with the garment industry. One of the most publicized disasters in the history of sweatshops occurred in 1911 at the Triangle Shirtwaist Factory on New York City's Lower East Side. A fire broke out in the cramped space where the workers sewed, and 146 women laborers were killed. While the tragedy led to improvements in domestic labor laws, sweatshops continue to thrive in many parts of the world.

With more fluid lines in women's fashions, undergarments had to be redesigned. Gone were the whalebone corsets that laced up tight enough to affect one's circulation and stiff petticoats worn in layers. They were replaced by bloomers and slips. Hats continued to be a fashion "necessity," but they, too, were simplified. The final year for huge, cumbersome hats sporting feathers and even exotic birds was 1910. After that, most hats were smaller and either turban-shaped or geometric-shaped.

By mid-decade, women were so comfortable in their daywear that they stopped the custom of changing into dinner dresses each evening. Parisian fashion designers such as Paul Poiret, Mademoiselle Paquin, and the Callot Soeurs (sisters) were offended by the turn in women's fashion away from the formal towards the functional. The French designers offered the "hobble-skirted" suit. It resembled the shape that would be adopted for the Coca-Cola bottle in 1916. This design, which restricted the length of a woman's stride, failed to sell, however. American designers countered with the popular "suffragette suit," which had a slit to allow for long steps. Rather than lose their clientele of wealthy American women, the French adjusted their styles to an understated look. After World War I, American tastes ran towards the new, sportier French designers, including Gabrielle "Coco" Chanel, Jean Patou, and Madeleine Vionnet.

❖ MEN'S CLOTHING REVOLVES AROUND THE SUIT; CHILDREN'S WEAR ADDS A PLAYTIME LINE

Clothing for men also reflected changes in lifestyle. With central heating newly installed in homes and offices, men no longer needed to wear bulky one-piece union suits as underwear during cold weather. Instead, they sleeked down their underwear to undershorts and a sleeveless undershirt. Soon men's suits were slimmed down to accommodate the new, less bulky line. Shoulder pads were thinned, and trousers became more fitted, ending in a cuff (a turned-back hem). Vests, still called waistcoats, were worn, as well as neckwear such as bow ties and ascots (scarves folded under the chin). Detachable, stiff shirt collars still were stylish. Since these were the days before elastic and spandex, garters were used to hold up socks.

Suits generally were made of woolen fabrics. Men wore lighter-weight woolens in warm seasons. Oxford tie shoes replaced high-button shoes that had to be buttoned shut with a special hook. Hats changed with the seasons. Braided straw "boaters" were fashionable in summer, and brimmed fedoras and rounded derbies were worn during the remainder of the seasons. In place of the pocket watch, the wristwatch was introduced in 1914. During the war, wearing a belt became fashionable, replacing the suspenders that men had worn to keep their trousers up. After the war, men adopted the military style trenchcoat, made by the British design house of Burberry.

The Norfolk jacket, allegedly based on a hunting jacket worn by an eighteenth-century Duke of Norfolk, became the jacket of choice for middle- and upper-class leisure activities such as golf and horseback riding. The jacket was fitted with a yolk (a shaped piece of fabric at the shoulders). With it, men wore knickers (shorter pants gathered at the knee) for golfing, and custom pants for other activities. Ankle-length topcoats, a fashion started by Harvard students in 1910, grew in acceptance as the decade progressed, particularly since the coats were practical for automobile driving. At the time, many roads were unpaved, and trouser legs might easily be dirtied by mud.

At the beginning of the decade, children mainly wore miniature versions of adult fashions. Poor children usually wore remade hand-me-downs from their parents' wardrobe. During World War I, ready-to-wear manufacturers began producing children's play clothes. They provided girls with the "gym slip," which consisted of loose, knee-length bloomers and tunic tops. For playtime, boys began wearing knee-length pants with knee socks and open-collar shirts. Following in the fashion of adults, all children wore hats in public.

Newspaper boys wearing popular 1910s fashions, including knee-length pants, knee socks, and caps. Reproduced by permission of the Corbis Corporation.

BOOKS

Andryszewski, Tricia. *Immigration: Newcomers and Their Impact on the United States.* Brookfield, CT: Millbrook Press, 1995.

Archer, James. *They Had a Dream: The Civil Rights Struggle from Frederick Douglass to Marcus Garvey to Martin Luther King to Malcolm X.* New York: Viking, 1993.

Bolden, Tonya, ed. *33 Things Every Girl Should Know About Women's History: From Suffragettes to Skirt Lengths to the E.R.A.* New York: Crown Publishing, 2002.

Boulton, Alexander O. *Frank Lloyd Wright, Architect: An Illustrated Biography.* New York: Rizzoli, 1993.

Carter, David A. *George Santayana.* New York: Chelsea House, 1992.

Davis, Frances A. *Frank Lloyd Wright: Maverick Architect.* Minneapolis: Lerner Publications, 1996.

Gourley, Catherine. *Good Girl Work: Sweatshops, and How Women Changed Their Role in the American Workforce.* Brookfield, CT: Millbrook Press, 1999.

Hoag, Edwin, and Joy Hoag. *Masters of Modern Architecture: Frank Lloyd Wright, Le Corbusier, Mies van der Rohe, and Walter Gropius.* Indianapolis: Bobbs-Merrill, 1977.

Kessler-Harris, Alice. *Women Have Always Worked: A Historical Overview.* New York: Feminist Press at the City University of New York, 1981.

Lawler, Mary. *Marcus Garvey.* New York: Chelsea House, 1988.

Rubin, Susan Goldman. *Frank Lloyd Wright.* New York: Harry N. Abrams, 1994.

Simonds, Christopher. *The Model T Ford.* Englewood Cliffs, NJ: Silver Burdett Press, 1991.

Williard, Charlotte. *Frank Lloyd Wright: American Architect.* New York: Macmillan, 1972.

WEB SITES

American Cultural History: The Twentieth Century, 1910–1919. http://www.nhmccd.cc.tx.us/contracts/lrc/kc/decade10.html (accessed on August 2, 2002).

Joe Hill. http://www.pbs.org/joehill/ (accessed on August 2, 2002).

Nobel e-Museum. John Raleigh Mott-Biography. http://www.nobel.se/peace/laureates/1946/mott-bio.html (accessed on August 2, 2002).

1910: A report by Abraham Flexner condemns the inadequate standards of many American medical schools, resulting in the closing of several schools and the merging of others.

1910: The hospital at the Rockefeller Institute opens.

1910: The National Association for the Study and Prevention of Infant Mortality is organized, leading to the opening of clinics for babies.

1910: Columbia University offers the first course in optics (science dealing with the origins of light) and optometry (profession of examining the eye for faults that are treatable through corrective lenses) in the United States.

1910: **October 3** The Ohio College of Dental Surgery in Cincinnati offers the first U.S. course for dental assistants and nurses.

1911: Measles is found to be a viral infection.

1912: The National Organization for Public Health Nursing is founded.

1912: Vitamin A is identified.

1912: The Sherley Amendment to the 1906 Pure Food and Drug Act challenges fraudulent claims of the effectiveness of patent medicines (nonprescription drugs protected by trademarks).

1912: French-born surgeon Alexis Carrel is the first American to win the Nobel Prize in medicine for suturing, or tying together, blood vessels.

1913: The American Cancer Society is organized.

1913: Mammography, an X-ray process for detecting breast cancer, is developed.

1913: Pellagra, a disease that would become associated with a deficiency of niacin and protein in the diet, claims 1,192 victims in Mississippi.

1913: The United States Children's Bureau publishes a pamphlet on prenatal care.

1913: **November 13** The first annual convention of the American College of Surgeons occurs in Chicago.

1914: The pasteurization of milk is instituted in large cities.

1914: The Life Extension Institute, an insurance organization, offers preventive health examinations.

1914: The Mayo family opens its Mayo Clinic building in Rochester, Minnesota.

1914: **June 22** The American College of Surgeons admits its first female members.

1915: The United States Public Health Service Division of Industrial Hygiene and Sanitation is organized.

1916: An epidemic of polio (a viral infection that results in fever, paralysis, and muscle atrophy) breaks out, striking more than twenty-eight thousand victims. Six thousand die, and many more are permanently crippled.

1916: The practice of refrigerating blood for transfusions is instituted.

1916: The National Board of Medical Examiners holds its initial examinations in Washington, D.C.

1916: **June 5** The U.S. Supreme Court rules that people who use or sell opium (an addictive narcotic drug made from the juice of the opium poppy) can be prosecuted.

1916: **October 16** Margaret Sanger opens the first birth control clinic in Brooklyn, New York.

1917: Vitamin D is isolated from cod-liver oil.

1917: **February 23** The American Society of Orthodontists is incorporated. Its members deal with irregularities of the teeth and treatment through braces.

1917: **June** The House of Delegates of the AMA approves a report that endorses health insurance.

1918: The AMA increases the prerequisite for entrance into a Class A medical school from one to two years of college.

1918: Congress passes the Chamberlain-Kahn Act for the study and control of venereal disease (a contagious disease contracted through sexual intercourse with an infected person).

1918: The American College of Surgeons institutes a program to evaluate hospital standards.

1918: **August 27** The "Spanish" flu epidemic begins in the United States with the diagnosis of two sailors in Boston.

1919: Ohio passes the first law for statewide care of handicapped children.

1919: **February 27** The American Association for the Hard of Hearing, a national social organization for the deaf and hearing-impaired, is formed in New York City.

1919: **December 23** The *Relief,* the first ambulance ship, is launched as a floating hospital.

Overview

In the spirit of social reform that characterized the Progressive Era, the 1910s saw many developments in public health education. It also was a time for new diagnostic and surgical techniques and advances in the use of medicines and treatments. In the midst of so many improvements, however, the single most memorable health-related story is the "Spanish" influenza epidemic of 1918 and 1919. This infectious flu swept through Europe, Asia, and North America, affecting hundreds of millions and actually killing 21.6 million people, more than 1 percent of the entire world population. In the United States, fear overtook American cities, and lifestyles were altered to avoid spread of the disease. Americans were afraid to gather in public places; many isolated themselves in their homes. The atmosphere was reminiscent of the plague, the deadly disease that spread through Europe during the Middle Ages (500–c. 1500). Schools were closed, theaters were shut down, parades were canceled. People hid their faces behind facial masks to avoid inhaling germs. When the epidemic subsided, more than five hundred thousand Americans were dead. No medical researchers have yet figured out why or how the "Spanish" influenza epidemic ended.

Many lives were also claimed throughout the decade by pneumonia and tuberculosis. Yet, with improved treatments, mortality (death) rates decreased. Due to the efforts of the U.S. Public Health Service (USPHS), there was a widespread campaign to educate Americans about the causes of particular illnesses and the newly available treatments for various sicknesses. There also were improved facilities and equipment, better trained doctors, and health insurance to allow working-class people access to expensive treatments formerly reserved for the wealthy.

Medical researchers continued to unlock many secrets about the causes of illnesses, which resulted in identifying proper steps for prevention as well as effective treatments. Paul Ehrlich, a German bacteriologist (one who studies microscopic plants) and immunologist (one who studies the body's responses to antibodies) discovered the compound salvarsan, which stopped the venereal disease syphilis from spreading through the body. It also was a pioneering drug used in chemotherapy treatment of cancer patients. Even so, the nation continued to be plagued by venereal disease (illness that spreads from sexual intercourse with an infected person). The USPHS, with a staff of expert "germ hunters," assigned scientists to make studies of diseases that were ravaging regions of the country. As a result, the lives of thousands were saved from potentially fatal illnesses such as pellagra and hookworm. Although USPHS scientists also investigated outbreaks of polio, it would be several more decades before that crippling disease was eradicated. As is still true, cancer was prevalent, particularly stomach and skin cancer, and breast and uterine (womb) cancer among women. Treatments for cancer were quite primitive, as was the public's understanding of the illness.

Treatments of all sorts of diseases improved as new hospitals and clinics were opened across the nation. On the East Coast, large hospitals featured staffs of well-trained physicians and many newly designed machines. In the Midwest, group practices of several physicians and a shared business and support staff were appearing in many cities, making sophisticated medical treatment affordable to the working class. The Mayo brothers set the standard for group practice with their world-famous clinic in Rochester, Minnesota.

The experiences of doctors during World War I (1914–18) helped medical professionals learn more about the state of health in America. Medical examinations on young male recruits revealed to doctors that many young Americans were suffering from physical conditions that could have been avoided through hygienic lifestyles and early and accessible medical treatment. They also found out that many young men were unfit for long marches carrying heavy backpacks and other military-related strength and endurance tests. As a result of the findings, physical education classes were added to public school programs across the country. Sometimes lifesaving breakthroughs come from adversity, and that certainly was the case with wartime medical advances during the 1910s. As American soldiers were wounded by enemy bullets and grenades, physicians at field hospitals near the front and in more formal hospitals back home developed new operating techniques to repair broken and shattered bodies. They introduced new surgical methods to avoid excessive blood loss and clear up infections. These advances later became standard procedures in civilian hospitals.

Fraudulent claims in the patent medicine industry continued to be a problem. Over-the-counter drugs containing addictive drugs, alcohol, and codeine were sold to millions of Americans, often to women for themselves and their infant children and sometimes with fatal results. These medicines claimed to cure all sorts of ailments from the common cold to "female problems" to cancer. Government legislation called for stricter guidelines in labeling and the American Medical Association (AMA), which took a growing role in the structure of the American medical industry, pressured manufacturers to use more honesty in their advertising.

Edward Calvin Kendall (1886–1972) With a Ph.D. in chemistry from Columbia University, Edward Calvin Kendall spent years researching matters relating to the thyroid hormone (a natural secretion of the endocrine gland that acts as a chemical messenger) of the thyroid gland. In 1915, he succeeded in isolating and chemically identifying the pure crystalline thyroid hormone, a breakthrough in the treatment of thyroid disorders. Then Kendall joined the Mayo Clinic staff, where he investigated the Compound E hormone (which was renamed cortisone). Cortisone became an effective treatment for rheumatoid arthritis, a crippling disease of pain, stiffness, and swelling of the joints. Its application allowed debilitated sufferers to regain the ability to walk and move more freely. *Photo courtesy of the Library of Congress.*

William Mayo (1861–1939) and Charles Mayo (1865–1939) In 1915, physicians and brothers William and Charles Mayo founded the Mayo Clinic as a surgical clinic in Rochester, Minnesota. One of America's first approaches to practicing medicine through teamwork, the Mayo clinic would become a world-renowned full-service medical center. During World War I (1914–18), "Dr. Will" and "Dr. Charlie" were among the chief advisers to the government regarding medical matters. Both men received the U.S. Distinguished Service Medal after the war. With their donation of a $1.5 million endowment in 1915, they also founded the Mayo Foundation for Medical Education and Research at the University of Minnesota. *Photo reproduced by permission of the Corbis Corporation.*

Adolf Meyer (1866–1950) A native of Switzerland, psychiatric theorist Adolf Meyer trained in at the University of Zurich before finding employment in the United States. Studying the work of American philosophers and psychologists, Meyer came up with a concept of human behavior that he called ergasiology or psychobiology, integrating the results of studies of psychology (the study of the mind) and biology (the study of life and living processes). From 1914 to 1941, he was director of the Henry Phipps Psychiatric Clinic at the Johns Hopkins University School of Medicine, one of the most significant training grounds for psychiatrists. Meyer helped to standardize the method of recording case histories of patients. He also reformed state asylums and was cofounder of a hygiene movement. *Photo reproduced by permission of the Corbis Corporation.*

Thomas Hunt Morgan (1866–1945) After obtaining a Ph.D. in comparative anatomy and physiology from Johns Hopkins University in 1890, Thomas Hunt Morgan became a professor of biology and zoology. In 1909, he began his extensive experimentation in genetics. Through laboratory work with fruit flies, Morgan was able to unlock many mysteries of heredity. He proved that units of heredity, called genes, were arranged in a line on chromosomes ("colored bodies" found in the nuclei of cells). Morgan's work established the chromosome as the storehouse of hereditary substance passed from one cell to another, and by parent to child, from generation to generation. In 1933, he was awarded the Nobel Prize for physiology or medicine for establishing that chromosomes carry hereditary traits. *Photo courtesy of the Library of Congress.*

Margaret Sanger (1879–1966) Activist Margaret Sanger is the single most important force behind the introduction and distribution of birth control methods in the United States. She also helped to remove the stigma of birth control. In her work as a nurse and midwife, she encountered many women who sought methods to restrict pregnancies. Despite a culture that condemned open discussions of sexual matters, Sanger began lecturing and writing articles on sex education and health. She founded the National Birth Control League in 1914 and the Planned Parenthood Foundation of America in 1921. In 1950, she sponsored research that led to the development of the birth control pill. *Photo reproduced by permission of the Corbis Corporation.*

Lillian D. Wald (1867–1940) While a student at the Woman's Medical College in New York, Lillian D. Wald became acquainted with the shockingly poor health conditions endured by tenement dwellers. She left school and cofounded the Henry Street Visiting Nurse Service on the Lower East Side, where she and colleagues provided health care for the neighborhood. In 1912, she helped persuade Congress to found the United States Children's Bureau for prenatal and maternal care of women with inadequate resources to pay for medical attention during their pregnancies. Wald also created the Rural Nursing Bureau of the American Red Cross. Her efforts laid the foundation for training programs in public health nursing, resulting in improved health conditions for generations of needy people. *Photo reproduced courtesy of Library of Congress.*

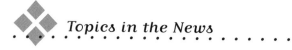

Topics in the News

❖ THE "SPANISH" FLU EPIDEMIC CLAIMS MILLIONS OF LIVES

An influenza epidemic struck the East Coast of the United States in September 1918, lasting for several months. This contagious disease had origins in China but was called the "Spanish" flu because it had raged in Spain before spreading to other countries in Europe and the United States. Symptoms included sneezing, runny nose, chills, high fever, muscle and joint aches, and general weakness. So potentially deadly was this virus that it eventually would kill 21.6 million people around the world. This was 1 percent of the world's population. Although the majority of Americans who contracted this sickness recovered, more than five hundred thousand Americans died from the "Spanish" influenza during 1918 and 1919.

The speed by which the infections and fatalities occurred were so high that no medical experts could stop the flu from taking its course. Attempts were made to keep people from congregating in order to halt the spread of the disease. Schools were closed and meetings were canceled. Soldiers crowded into military camps were particularly susceptible to the flu. Many people wore masks over their noses and mouths to prevent picking up this contagious disease from friends and coworkers. Although it was not rare to have outbreaks of influenza in the United States, none before had affected one in every four people. During 1919, the epidemic subsided, but nobody knows how such a powerful and destructive virus disappeared so abruptly.

❖ THE GROWING ACCEPTANCE OF GROUP PRACTICE IN MEDICINE

During the 1910s, the concept of structuring doctors into private group practice began in the Midwest. According to this plan, private clinics or medical centers were formed with doctors as owners and employees. They also included business managers and office and technical staff. Under this economically efficient system, several doctors could share the responsibility for purchasing expensive equipment. Without paying higher fees, patients had access to the expertise of several physicians in sophisticated facilities. The movement grew at a fairly steady rate from 1914 to the end of the decade.

One of the most prominent of these pioneering group practices was the Mayo Clinic, which opened a new building in Rochester, Minnesota, in 1914. Two brothers who were surgeons, William Mayo (1861–1939) and Charles

Prestigious Awards in Medicine and Pharmacology

Nobel Prize Winner in Physiology or Medicine

1912   Alexis Carrel (1873–1944) for transplantation and suturing (tying together) of blood vessels.

The Ebert Prize

The Ebert Prize is awarded for the best original paper published during the preceding year in the *Journal of Pharmaceutical Sciences* (the sciences of drugs such as toxins and therapeutics). It first was given in 1874.

1910	Harry M. Gordin
1911	W.A. Puckner with L.E. Warren
1912	No award
1913	No award
1914	No award
1915	E.N. Gathercoal
1916	John Uri Lloyd
1917	No award
1918	No award
1919	No award

The Remington Honor Medal

The Remington Honor Medal is given annually for the best work in American pharmacy during the year, or to an individual whose work over a period has advanced the pharmaceutical field. It first was awarded in 1919 to James Hartley Beal.

Mayo (1865–1939), brought together an expert staff of surgeons, diagnosticians (those who identify disease from symptoms), and medical researchers from across the United States and foreign countries. The following year, the brothers donated $1.5 million to endow the Mayo Foundation for Medical Education and Research at the University of Minnesota. The Mayos were a family of physicians. In 1889, their father, William Worrall Mayo (1819–1911), had founded St. Mary's Hospital in Rochester, Minnesota, as an emergency hospital to treat victims of a cyclone (a wind storm). From this seed would come one of the most significant group practices in the world.

The success of the Mayo Clinic sparked the development of private group practices in cities throughout the Midwest and Far West. Even so, the concept never became popular in the East because expansive hospitals with large staffs of affiliated physicians already had mushroomed in cities.

Although the concept of group practice had a huge following among doctors, many physicians preferred to remain in individual private practices. They argued that group practices were impersonal and their fees were undercutting the standard rates. As the decade closed, the spread of group practices started to slow. This slowdown was due to the sharp increase in sophisticated and costly medical technology following World War I (1914–18), which could be dealt with only within the structure of huge hospital centers.

❖ AMERICAN REFORMERS SEEK BROAD HEALTH INSURANCE COVERAGE

As the decade unfolded, very few members of the working class were covered by health insurance policies. Laborers often purchased life insurance in order to ensure a proper funeral; however, the few who were insured against medical crises were covered not by their employer but by small brotherhoods or local chapters of unions. The first legislation related to health insurance dealt with workers' compensation, payments that would be made to workers who were injured while on the job. In 1911, the first workers' compensation law was enacted by the Wisconsin legislature. By 1915, about twenty states had passed similar legislation.

Still, there was little effort to insure people against the cost of paying for sickness and disabilities unrelated to their work. In 1907, the newly founded American Association of Labor Legislation (AALL) had called for social improvements for workers, including insurance against illness. In 1915, the AALL worked to introduce a bill into state legislatures calling for compulsory health insurance for workers who earned less than $1,200 per year, as well as for other employees who wanted to buy into a health insurance program. During 1916, a number of states did try to pass bills for health insurance and other social-oriented insurances. Among the detractors was Samuel Gompers (1850–1924), president of the American Federation of Labor (AFL), who did not support government intervention in matters that he believed could be handled by trade unions and employers.

During 1917, arguments raged among various groups who disagreed about the best approach to bringing health care to the American public. Many social reformers urged passage of compulsory health insurance laws, similar to laws that had passed previously first in Germany, and later in

Great Britain. In January 1917, the *Journal of the American Medical Association* published editorials in favor of the compulsory health insurance program. Soon after, those reformers began citing the economic structure of group practices as the solution to obtaining affordable, widespread health care. That support placed that group of reformers at odds with individual physicians who were striving to retain the single doctor practice, and the resulting political fray led the American Medical Association (AMA) to change its stance and come out against compulsory health insurance policies. When the United States entered World War I in April 1917, the move towards government-supported health insurance further subsided. By then, any movement that was connected to Germany was considered unpatriotic. Furthermore, a Red Scare arose in the United States at the end of the decade. This fear of the rise of communism (a system of government by which the state controls the economy and a single party holds power) overtook many Americans and government health insurance programs were considered too "red," or communist, in their collective approach to protecting society for acceptance by the United States.

❖ THE EFFECTS OF WORLD WAR I ON THE MEDICAL PROFESSION

In 1916, President Woodrow Wilson (1856–1924) began to prepare the nation to meet the medical needs that would result if the country had to enter the war in Europe. In so doing, he appointed a Council of National Defense (CND) with a medical division. Three surgeons general of the Army, Navy, and the U.S. Public Health Service served on the CND's executive committee, along with several of the country's most prominent physicians. It was their task to plan a strategy to handle the many medical situations that war breeds.

At the start of the recruitment process, doctors performed thousands of health examinations on young Americans who were about to join the military. To their surprise, they learned that many were in poor health. They lacked the stamina to pass physical tests required of soldiers, such as doing push-ups and running. Having never been checked before, the recruits were found to suffer from poor hygiene (the science of cleanliness to maintain health) and poor nutrition. Recruits from rural areas in particular were suffering from undiagnosed cases of venereal disease (illness that spreads from sexual intercourse with an infected person), which could have been treated to lessen the long-term damage of the disease. As a result of finding so many Americans lacking in health care, states instituted programs that called for physical examinations in public schools as early as kindergarten. Schools also began to emphasize the importance of physical education classes to improve strength and endurance levels among American youngsters.

Even the healthy recruits faced the dangers of communicable diseases (contagious sicknesses that could be passed from one person to another through close contact). As tens of thousands of soldiers were crowded into the country's thirty-two military training camps, healthy recruits became ill due to outbreaks of measles, mumps, cerebro-spinal (meningococcal) meningitis (a bacterial disease involving inflammation of three membranes wrapping the brain and spinal cord), and typhoid fever (a bacterial disease marked by fever and inflamed intestines). The highest death rates in camps were caused by pneumonia and the "Spanish" influenza epidemic.

When one considers the causes of wartime fatalities, it is routine to picture armed soldiers being killed by bullets and grenades. However, during World War I, 21,053 American soldiers died of pneumonia resulting from cases of the flu in late 1918. During the winter of 1917 and 1918, pneumonia, contracted as the result of having other communicable diseases, caused 3,110 deaths. Measles had been thought of as a minor childhood disease, and it would have been less significant an illness had it not been for the fact that it weakened men's immune systems. It reduced their resistance to other

Wounded American soldiers during World War I were transported by American Red Cross ambulances. The fact that these ambulances could be driven right up to the trenches to pick up the wounded helped to contribute to the survival of many soldiers. Reproduced by permission of the Corbis Corporation.

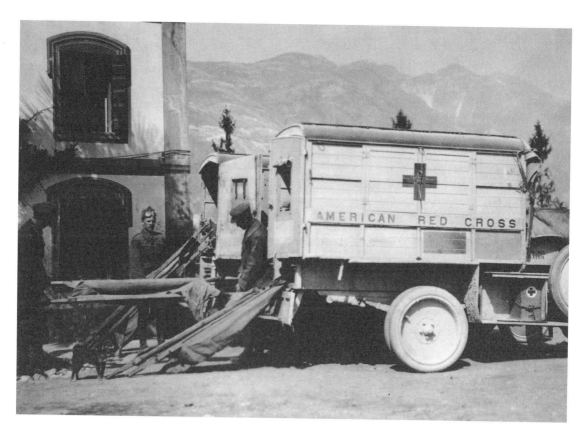

The

GREATEST MOTHER
in the WORLD

A poster for the American Red Cross of a World War I nurse and a wounded soldier. Besides being wounded during combat, soldiers also had to worry about catching various diseases during wartime. **Courtesy of the Library of Congress.**

bacterial infections. For every 1,000 men who contracted measles, 44 got pneumonia, leading to an average of 14 fatalities.

Combat wounds caused 53,400 deaths. Due to improvements in surgical techniques, as many as 204,000 wounded soldiers survived the war. Additionally, X rays (electromagnetic radiation of wavelengths) helped doctors identify problems, tetanus antitoxin injections helped to clear

How Cancer Was Treated

In 1913, cancer was among the top six causes of death in the United States. In certain regions of the country, it was surpassed only by pneumonia and tuberculosis. At the time, weight loss and general weakness were considered the symptoms of cancer, and pain was believed to be a sign of the disease in its late stages. Early detection and surgery were the only known means of treating the affliction.

According to an article written by Samuel Hopkins Adams (1871–1958) in the May 1913 issue of the *Ladies' Home Journal,* specialists were urging the public to be educated about cancer, and to self-examine in order to locate tumors. The leading cancer was stomach cancer, which was operable in 1913, although only one third of those who had surgery survived. Forms of skin cancer also were operable. For women, breast and uterine cancer were common enemies. If cancerous tumors were located in the early stages, they could be removed through surgery, with varying survival rates.

In his 1913 article, Adams mentioned three "facts" about cancer, all of which were considered true at the time: "First, cancer usually develops from previous and continued irritation. Second, if the cause of that irritation [can] be removed in time the cancer will be averted. Third, if the development of cancer [can] be determined in the early stages the patient can probably be cured by operation, but not by any other method." These "facts" sound quaint to readers in the twenty-first century, since cancer knowledge is far more sophisticated and there are many options for treating cancers, including radiation, chemotherapy, and improved surgical techniques.

infections, and blood transfusions replaced lost blood to help soldiers heal. The use of motorized ambulance vehicles that could be driven right up to the trenches to pick up the wounded also contributed to the survival of many soldiers.

One of the least understood injuries of World War I was shell shock, a condition of modern warfare caused by the vacuum created by bursting shells. When air rushes into this vacuum, it upsets the function of the brain. Symptoms include dizziness, temper tantrums, headaches, fatigue, and the inability to concentrate. Eventually, those suffering from shell shock experienced mental breakdowns. At the time, it was suggested that

the cure for the illness was complete rest and relaxation far away from battle, and shell-shock victims spent months and even years in mental asylums. Many others suffering from shell shock were mistakenly labeled
cowards and malingerers who wished only to avoid combat. Many sufferers were dispatched back into battle. Some committed suicide. Others
deserted. Still more disobeyed orders and were shot on the spot or court-
martialed. The British Army estimated that as many as 80,000 soldiers suffered from shell shock during the war.

Treatments developed to cure war injuries became standard medical
practices in postwar civilian health care. The use of chlorine and the
"Carrel-Dakin" approach to flushing wounds with Dakin fluid (a noncaus-
tic hypochloride) proved to be a significant medical advance for treating
infected wounds. Also, the spread of communicable diseases during the
war led medical researchers to discover treatments for some illnesses, such
as typhoid fever, lock-jaw (an early form of tetanus, which is an acute
infectious disease involving spasms of voluntary muscles in the jaw),
pneumonia, and meningitis.

❖ THE GOVERNMENT CONFRONTS MATTERS OF PUBLIC HEALTH

During the Progressive Era of the first two decades of the century,
American social reformers strived to implement new advances in medical
science and technology to improve the general state of the public's health.
First in 1902, and again in 1912, Congress passed legislation to expand
the nation's first bacteriological laboratory at the Staten Island (New York)
Marine Hospital. The 1912 legislation called for medical research,
improved methods of public health administration, federal funding for
state and local health departments, and interstate control of sanitation and
communicable diseases.

By 1914, every state except New Mexico and Wyoming had set up public health laboratories in conjunction with state boards of health. The staffs
of these laboratories coordinated efforts with physicians and public health
officers to distribute vaccines and other medicines, and helped to diagnose
outbreaks of communicable diseases. Until late in the decade, most public
health work was done on a grassroots level. In 1918, the Chamberlain-
Kahn Act, providing for the study and control of venereal disease, became
the first significant instance of a federal appropriation for public health.

Early training in public health was offered in 1913 in a joint program
from Harvard Medical School and the Massachusetts Institute of Technology (MIT). In 1918, the first separate Institute of Hygiene and Public

Health was established at Johns Hopkins University. The degree was geared to doctors intending to work in the public health sector. It called for knowledge of sanitation, immunization, vital statistics, and various contagious diseases.

In 1914, the USPHS made a study in the South of an outbreak of pellagra (a disease marked by skin and stomach disorders and symptoms related to the central nervous system, including dementia, in severe cases). Believing it to be an infectious disease, the service assigned microbe (germ) researcher Joseph Goldberger (1874–1929) to investigate. Goldberger chose inmates of the Rankin State Prison Farm in Mississippi as a test group. After a testing period, he came to the conclusion that the disease was caused by a dietary deficiency, not the spread of microorganisms. Eventually, by further testing, Goldberger learned that pellagra could be stopped by adding niacin and protein to the diet.

USPHS research zoologist (scientist dealing with the study of animal life) Charles Wardell Stiles (1867–1941) investigated an infestation of hookworm in the southern states. Hookworm stems from the presence of a worm within the intestinal tract. These worms hatch from the larvae of eggs in soil tainted by feces. Then the worms penetrate the skin of persons walking barefoot. Since many rural southerners were impoverished and wore no shoes, the worms found many unwitting hosts. Once in the intestines, the worms feed from the person's blood supply, causing anemia and sometimes death. If the host is a child, the result can be impairment to mental and physical development. With the sponsorship of the Rockefeller Sanitary Commission, Stiles studied five hundred thousand children in eleven southern states and found that 39 percent of the youngsters suffered from hookworm disease. Working with local and state health organizations, the USPHS administered a widespread clean up program in rural southern regions to prevent the disease from spreading further, and also treated the sick with thymol capsules.

Another area of public health that called for attention was the infant and mother mortality rate. Thousands of babies died every year due to poor prenatal care, and mothers died while giving birth due to unhealthy birthing practices. By 1915, 538 baby clinics were running in the United States. These clinics offered medical care and education for pregnant mothers. Mothers learned about proper hygiene, good life habits, and healthy diets.

❖ PATENT MEDICINES BECOME A MORE HONEST BUSINESS

Shortly after the century began, the packaged or nonprescription patent medicine market was estimated to be a $75 million to $100

During World War I, German American chemist Ernst Mahler (1887–1967) invented an absorbent wood-cellulose substitute for cotton called "Cellucotton" to be used for bandaging at field hospitals near the trenches. Soon Red Cross nurses began using this bandaging in wads for menstrual pads. In 1921, the Kimberly-Clark Corporation, with whom Mahler was associated, began marketing the first widely sold disposable sanitary napkins made of Cellucotton. They were named "Kotex," short for *cot*ton-like *texture*.

Advertised as "inexpensive, comfortable, hygienic and safe," Kotex cost five cents per napkin, or a dozen for sixty cents. Since the subject of menstruation was taboo, Kotex came in unmarked wrappers and could be purchased discreetly by dropping coins in a box, instead of having to deal with a store clerk.

million-per-year business. This industry had spun out of control, with dangerous consequences. Unsuspecting customers, particularly women, were purchasing pills, powders, and syrups to cure all ailments, from coughs, aches, "female problems," and infant discomforts to cancer. Since labels often listed no ingredients or false ingredients, the customer was ignorant of taking such components as alcohol and codeine, or even addictive narcotics such as morphine, heroin, and opium. Many of these medicines were debilitating when used over long periods, and some became killers when overdoses were administered.

The Pure Food and Drug Act of 1906 was enacted by Congress to clean up abuses in the patent medicine industry. This legislation helped to clarify ingredients and also made sure that patent medicines were produced in hygienic environments. Still, over-the-counter medicines continued to boast many fraudulent claims, and "quack" cures were prevalent. In 1912, the Sherley Amendment made fraudulent claims illegal. However, by placing the burden of proof on the government rather than the medicine manufacturers, the legislation was ineffective. Eventually, the American Medical Association (AMA) campaigned against false advertising of patent medicines in newspapers, leading to more honest advertisements. For example, for many years the Pinkham Company had marketed its vegetable compound to treat such "female complaints" as bloating, irregular menstruation, and a prolapsed uterus (fallen or slipped womb), and kidney complaints in both sexes. However, by 1915 the AMA had convinced Pinkham to sell its products with more general claims.

The AMA criticized drug companies for charging high prices for inexpensively produced patent medicines. For instance, the Bayer Company, the original producer of aspirin, was making questionable claims that their "Aspirin-Bayer" was expensive to produce. In 1917, the AMA was so incensed over Bayer's stance that they waged a campaign to prevent the company from renewing its proprietary patent on aspirin. As a result, Bayer's patent was not renewed, meaning the company lost its control of the market. After 1917, aspirin could be manufactured and sold by any company that wanted to enter the marketplace.

While it was fighting false claims of patent medicines and quack treatments, the AMA also was encouraging the public to entrust its medical needs to licensed physicians. The campaign was beneficial in preventing the uninformed public from buying useless or dangerous products. At the same time, the AMA was working to empower the trained medical profession to set the standards for treatments and cures by replacing many patent medicines with prescription medicines.

❖ ADVANCED TECHNIQUES IN SURGERY AND THE USE OF X RAYS

Harvey Williams Cushing (1869–1939) was one of the outstanding neurosurgeons (brain and spinal cord surgeons) of the period. In 1907, he developed a process of using small silver clamps to stop excessive blood loss during brain surgery, resulting in a much higher operation success rate. By the start of the 1910s, he had achieved an astounding 90 percent reduction rate in brain surgery deaths. During World War I, Cushing's procedure saved the lives of many wounded combat soldiers. He also adapted his innovative surgical techniques for use in removing metal shell fragments from the brain with the help of a large magnet. The magnet's pull identified the location of the metal and helped to force the metal from the brain.

Wounds resulting from the violent battles of trench warfare sometimes left soldiers with terrible facial and limb disfigurement. To treat these victims, British and French surgeons came up with new techniques in reconstructive surgery. New York surgeon F. H. Albee (1876–1945) introduced a procedure to graft bone from healthy parts of the body onto damaged parts in order to make repairs. Using new techniques, doctors could help a soldier whose nose had been shot off, if only a bit of loose skin remained in the middle of his face. Doctors could "grow" a new nose for the victim by stretching the remaining skin little by little over a set period, and then grafting bone from the victim's wrist onto his face where it eventually took hold. Not every disfigured soldier could be helped through surgery. Many held no hope of replacing shot-off cheeks, jaws, or noses. To help such individuals, French sculptors created wax face molds that covered part or all of a wounded man's face. Although the covering did not look quite natural, it saved the soldier from having to publicly display his disfigurement.

Early in the decade, surgeon Hugh H. Young (1870–1945) introduced advances in the field of urology (the science that deals with urinary and genital tract diseases). Young invented a "punch operation" to remove tumors from the male prostate gland. In 1912, he successfully performed this surgery on James Buchanan "Diamond Jim" Brady (1856–1917), a powerful railroad tycoon who was famous for being an extravagant spender. In gratitude, Brady gave generous funding to endow the James Buchanan Brady Urological Institute at Johns Hopkins Hospital.

As the 1910s began, X rays (electromagnetic radiation of wavelengths) already were in use as a means of diagnosis and therapy. In 1913, the first efficient X-ray tube was developed by William David Coolidge (1873–1975), replacing old-fashioned gas tubes. During World War I, "Coolidge tubes" were manufactured at the General Electric plant in Schenectady, New York, and sent to the European front for use in treating wounded soldiers. As with so many other wartime advances, the X ray became even more efficient through postwar developments for civilian use. Coolidge went on to become head of the research laboratory at General Electric from the early 1930s until the closing days of World War II (1939–45).

❖ THE TUBERCULOSIS MORTALITY RATE DECLINES

Tuberculosis spreads through bacterial infection. It is a highly contagious disease. If a person's white blood cell count cannot ward off the infection, then a victim will suffer lung tissue damage. Symptoms of the disease include coughing up blood, fever, weight loss, and tiredness. In 1906, tuberculosis killed one in every five hundred individuals in the United States. Throughout the 1910s, it caused more deaths than any other infectious disease.

Victims of tuberculosis were isolated and ordered to rest in sanatoriums. Sometimes these rests lasted months, as patients lay dormant, usually reading and sleeping. Treatment included the injection of nitrogen into one lung to make it collapse. That way, the collapsed or inactive lung might heal, while the second lung worked. This procedure, which never was properly evaluated, was called artificial pneumothorax. Fresh air and sunlight also were part of the treatment, so many sanitariums were located in resort areas or in the countryside. During the decade, there were approximately four hundred private, state, and municipal sanitariums in the United States. The National Tuberculosis Association lead a publicity campaign to inform the public about the disease and its dangers.

 For More Information

BOOKS

Bachrach, Deborah. *The Importance of Margaret Sanger.* San Diego: Lucent Books, 1993.

Benowitz, Steven I. *Cancer.* Berkeley Heights, NJ: Enslow Publishers, 1999.

Block, Irvin. *Neighbor to the World; the Story of Lillian Wald.* New York: Ty Crowell, 1969.

Hyde, Margaret O. *Know About Tuberculosis.* New York: Walker & Company, 1994.

Hyde, Margaret O., and Elizabeth H. Forsyth. *Vaccinations: From Smallpox to Cancer.* New York: Franklin Watts, 2000.

Landau, Elaine. *Tuberculosis.* New York: Franklin Watts, 1995.

McClafferty, Carla Killough. *The Head Bone's Connected to the Neck Bone: The Weird, Wacky, and Wonderful X-Ray.* New York: Farrar Strauss & Giroux, 2001.

Siegel, Beatrice. *Lillian Wald of Henry Street.* New York: Macmillan, 1983.

Silverstein, Alvin, Virginia Silverstein, and Robert Silverstein. *Measles and Rubella.* Springfield, NJ: Enslow Publishers, 1997.

Silverstein, Alvin, Virginia Silverstein, and Robert Silverstein. *Tuberculosis.* Hillside, NJ: Enslow Publishers, 1994.

Topalian, Elyse. *Margaret Sanger.* New York: Franklin Watts, 1984.

Whitelaw, Nancy. *Margaret Sanger: Every Child a Wanted Child.* New York: Dillon Press, 1994.

Yancey, Diane. *Tuberculosis.* Brookfield, CT: Twenty-First Century Books, 2001.

WEB SITES

The American Experience: Influenza 1918. http://www.pbs.org/wgbh/amex/influenza/ (accessed on August 2, 2002).

The Great War and the Shaping of the Twentieth Century. http://www.pbs.org/greatwar/ (accessed on August 2, 2002).

Nobel e-Museum. Edward Calvin Kendall-Biography. http://www.nobel.se/medicine/laureates/1950/kendall-bio.html (accessed on August 2, 2002).

Noble e-Museum. Thomas Hunt Morgan-Biography. http://www.nobel.se/medicine/laureates/1933/morgan-bio.html (accessed on August 2, 2002).

Science and Technology

1910: Electric washing machines become popular in American homes.

1910: Halley's Comet is observed "as a giant headlight" in the night sky across the United States.

1911: The Bell Telephone Company creates a research and development division.

1911: Physicists from across the world discuss recently developed atomic theories at the first Solvay conference, named for the Belgian industrial chemist and philanthropist who founded the Solvay Institute at Brussels, Belgium.

1911: The world's first escalators are introduced at London's Earl's Court underground (train) station.

1911: German American Franz Boas publishes *The Mind of Primitive Man,* a groundbreaking exploration of cultural anthropology (the study of human beings).

1911: The word "vitamin" is coined by Polish American biochemist Casimir Funk.

1911: **August 1** Harriet Quimby becomes the first licensed female pilot.

1911: **August 8** The U.S. Patent Office awards its one-millionth patent, for the invention of an improved automobile tire.

1911: **December 14** Norwegian explorer Roald Amundsen becomes the first person in history to reach the South Pole.

1912: The Morse Code SOS (Save Our Ship) is adopted as the universal signal for a ship at sea in distress.

1912: **April 14–15** The "unsinkable" steamship *Titanic* strikes an iceberg while on its maiden voyage and promptly sinks.

1913: Henry Ford introduces the assembly line, employed in the manufacturing of automobiles.

1913: Construction is completed on the Los Angeles aqueduct, which carries fresh water into the city from high in the Sierra Nevada mountains.

1913: Hungarian American Bela Schick develops the "Schick test" for diagnosing diphtheria (a disease characterized by inflammation of the heart and nervous system).

1913: Russian-born American aeronautical engineer Igor Sikorsky builds and flies the first multimotored airplane.

1913: French physicist Charles Fabry discovers the ozone layer in the Earth's stratosphere.

1914: Theodore Richards becomes the first American to win the Nobel Prize in chemistry.

1914: The first transcontinental telephone line is completed.

1914: The Boston Wire Stitcher Company introduces the modern staple gun.

1915: A new type of glass called Pyrex (8 percent silicon oxide and 12 percent boron oxide) is created at the Corning Glass Works in New York.

1915: An all-metal airplane is developed in Germany.

1915: German-born American physicist Albert Einstein discloses his general theory of relativity.

1915: January 25 Alexander Graham Bell, inventor of the telephone, completes the first transcontinental phone call, from New York to San Francisco.

1915: October The first transatlantic radiotelephone conversation is completed between the Eiffel Tower in Paris and Arlington, Virginia.

1916: German astronomer Karl Schwarzchild suggests the theoretical existence of "black holes" (intense gravitational fields in space, from which nothing, not even light, can escape).

1917: Dutch astronomer Willem de Sitter asserts that the universe is expanding.

1917: November 1 The Hooker Telescope, a reflecting telescope with a 100-inch mirror installed at the Mount Wilson Observatory in Pasadena, California, is used for the first time.

1918: The nation's first three-color traffic light (red, amber, green) is installed in New York City.

1919: Short-wave radio is invented, and amateur radio operators begin taking to the airwaves.

1919: A mechanical system for transmitting television pictures is patented.

1919: Lockheed produces the hydraulic braking system for automobiles.

1919: May 19 Astronomers confirm Albert Einstein's general theory of relativity by observing the bending of a star's light around the Sun during a total eclipse.

1919: June 14–15 John Alcock and Arthur Whitten-Brown make the first non-stop aerial crossing of the Atlantic Ocean.

1919: October The Radio Corporation of America (RCA) is founded.

Overview

The 1910s was notable for groundbreaking scientific research and startling discoveries that improved the general quality of life at the time and led to then-unimagined technological advances later in the twentieth century. Astronomers explored the skies in order to understand the nature of the universe. The world's largest telescope was constructed, allowing astronomers the opportunity to view several hundred million stars. The first synthetically produced plastic was invented and was commercially marketed in 1917. People thought of new uses for electricity. Improvements in the content of fertilizer modernized the farming industry. Geologists speculated on the origins of the Earth. In the biological sciences, researchers explored the composition of genes and how they are related to heredity. Electric refrigerators were marketed, which revolutionized the manner in which food was stored and preserved at the home. The link between food content and disease was acknowledged, and new laws and codes were passed to ensure that better-preserved edibles would be sold and consumed.

The decade saw the beginnings of commercial aviation. Airplane distance and speed records were established, and cross-country and transcontinental air flights were completed. Automobile manufacturing was becoming one of America's premier industries; the Ford Motor Company's Model T was the car of choice for drivers. In 1913, Henry Ford introduced the assembly line in his manufacturing plants, which resulted in a significant increase in auto production. Among the decade's innovations were the all-steel automobile body, front-mounted engine, and electric starter. Electric and steam-powered cars also were marketed, while trucks began replacing horse-drawn vehicles as a primary mode for transporting goods on roadways. Rapid advances were made in radio technology, including the amplification of radio waves and the invention of an efficient radio receiver.

A series of lectures presented in the United States by Austrian neurologist and psychiatrist Sigmund Freud led to an increased interest in psychoanalysis (a form of psychiatric examination that involves dream interpretation and an understanding of the ego, id, and superego). Meanwhile, physicists explored the nature of matter and the composition of the atom. German-born physicist Albert Einstein shook the physics community in 1916 with his groundbreaking general theory of relativity. In the simplest terms, this theory states that the nature of one entity is dependent on that of another.

Science and technology were not the exclusive domains of male pioneers. Among the women who made headlines with their accomplishments were airplane pilots Harriet Quimby and Ruth Law, astronomer Henrietta Leavitt, and biological scientist Louise Pearce.

As World War I (1914–18) raged through a good portion of the decade, science and invention helped to modernize the ways in which armies battled. Before the war, sonar (a mechanism that detected the presence of submerged objects) was employed to detect schools of fish. During the war, it was used to note the presence of enemy submarines. Among the tools of war invented or developed during the decade were lightweight machine guns, incendiary bombs, artillery shells, short- and long-range listening devices, flamethrowers, tanks, sea mines, and poison gases. Airplanes were commissioned to carry bombs. Some of the war's most celebrated combatants were pilots, whose participation in air battles made them instant heroes. Such uses of science and technology on the battlefield serve to illustrate that not all technological innovations are employed for the purpose of peace, prosperity, and advancing civilization.

Albert Einstein (1879–1955) German-born American physicist Albert Einstein is perhaps the twentieth century's most celebrated scientist. He electrified the physics community with his special theory of relativity in 1905 and his general theory of relativity in 1916. In the first, he speculated that space and time are not absolute, and are independent realities. The speed of light, however, is a constant in all frames of reference. His general theory extended his earlier work to account for systems moving relative to each other at any speed, even if those speeds are changing. Primarily, this theory centers on the large-scale effects of gravitation. *Photo reproduced by permission of AP/Wide World Photos.*

Robert Goddard (1882–1945) Robert Goddard's first trailblazing experiments in rocketry, the initial steps that led to the exploration of space, were conducted during the decade. In 1916 and 1917, he experimented with rockets fueled by solid chemical propellants, but found this means of propulsion unsatisfactory. In 1926, he and two assistants detonated the world's first liquid-fueled rocket. Upon America's entry into World War I (1914–18), Goddard developed small rockets to be used as weapons by the U.S. Army.

Irving Langmuir (1881–1957) Irving Langmuir, a General Electric researcher, was an all-purpose scientist. He made a significant contribution to the development of the modern lightbulb when he proved that adding inert gas to the bulb enhanced the life of its tungsten filament and made the bulb more energy efficient. His work on a mercury vacuum pump became a key development in the evolution of the radio tube. While investigating atomic structure, he was involved in groundbreaking research on electrically charged gases. During the decade, Langmuir began his studies of surface chemistry that led to his winning the 1932 Nobel Prize in chemistry. *Photo reproduced courtesy of Library of Congress.*

Henrietta Leavitt (1868–1921) While employed at the Harvard College Observatory astronomer Henrietta Leavitt established a method for ranking star magnitudes (numbers representing a celestial body's brightness) on photographic plates. She also discovered more variable stars (stars whose brightness periodically changes) than any other astronomer. In fact, the 2,400 variables she catalogued were about half the known variables at the time. In 1912, Leavitt ascertained the amount of time it takes for a Cepheid star to complete its bright-dim cycle. Such determinations were central to the eventual determination of intergalactic distances. *Photo reproduced by permission of the Granger Collection.*

Theodore Richards (1868–1928) Chemist Theodore Richards, a Harvard professor and researcher, was fascinated by the precise calculation of atomic weights. This interest led to his painstaking measurement of the atomic weight of water. Through his research, he proved that the ratio of oxygen to hydrogen in water was 15.869 (rather than 16, which had been the common belief). Previous measurements of certain chemicals, Richards found, had been calculated using impure samples. He also discovered that the atomic weight of lead that had been exposed to radioactive uranium differed from that of unexposed lead. For his work, Richards became the first American to be awarded the Nobel Prize in chemistry in 1914. *Photo reproduced courtesy of Library of Congress.*

Henry Russell (1877–1957) Princeton University professor Henry Russell was most celebrated for his groundbreaking work in the charting of stellar evolution. Drawing on the collective insights of previous astronomers, he challenged the accepted pattern of stellar development, which held that stars evolved from blue (hot) to red (cool). Russell concluded that red stars represented both the beginning and end of stellar evolution. He published his findings in 1913. *Photo reproduced by permission of the Corbis Corporation.*

Vesto Slipher (1875–1969) Vesto Slipher began his career as an assistant to the renowned astronomer and writer Percival Lowell (1855–1916). Under Lowell's guidance, Slipher searched for evidence of water and oxygen on Mars and measured the length of a day on Venus. He found that Uranus rotated once every 10.8 hours, and he determined the rotational periods of Mars, Jupiter, and Saturn. Slipher was among the first astronomers to offer evidence of the existence of interstellar gases and dust. He also completed research involving spiral nebulae (large bodies of dust or gas in space), observing that the majority of fourteen nebulae he had studied were receding from our solar system at high rates of speed. *Photo reproduced by permission of the Corbis Corporation.*

Alfred Sturtevant (1891–1970) Alfred Sturtevant was the first geneticist to realize that the frequency of crossing-over between genes is an index to the distance between them. This acknowledgment allowed him to produce the first basic genetic map. Additionally, he discovered that double crossing-over between genes can occur. While conducting experiments on fruit flies in the laboratory of the renowned geneticist Thomas Hunt Morgan (1866–1945), Sturtevant was able to trace inheritance patterns. This work served as the basis for much subsequent research into general genetic behavior.

Topics in the News

❖ THE AIRPLANE: SOARING INTO THE SKY

In 1903, the brothers Orville Wright (1871–1948) and Wilbur Wright (1867–1912) successfully flew the first aircraft at Kitty Hawk, North Carolina. However, America and the world did not immediately take to the air. It was not until the advent of World War I (1914–18) that airplanes began to be produced in mass quantities. And then, they mainly were used as tools of war, rather than for commercial purposes.

Even so, the prewar years saw a number of impressive achievements in aviation. In 1910, aviator Glenn Curtiss (1878–1930) set a new long-distance speed record when he flew from Albany, New York, to New York City in 150 minutes. Curtiss also developed the first seaplane, which featured pontoons instead of wheels. The initial cross-country air flight occurred between September 17 and November 5, 1911. The time spent in the air totaled three days and ten hours, with sixty-eight stops made along the way. Thirty were unscheduled. Harriet Quimby (1875–1912), a magazine editor, became the first woman licensed as a pilot, and Ruth Law (1887–1970) flew nonstop between Chicago and New York. The first scheduled airline flight took place on New Year's Day 1914, when American flier Tony Jannus (1889–1916) piloted a biplane between St. Petersburg and Tampa, Florida, carrying a single passenger.

In 1914, only five thousand airplanes existed in the entire world. However, at the outset of the war in Europe, military strategists realized that the airplane could help forces win battles, and as a result, planes were employed for surveying enemy territory and bombing. Loaded with machine guns, they could fly low and shoot enemy infantry at close range. The first dog-fights (one-on-one battles between two or more planes equipped with guns) captured the imaginations of Americans. Germany's Baron Manfred von Richtofen (1892–1918), popularly known as the Red Baron, was involved in eighty successful dogfights before being killed in action. French pilot Rene Fonck (1894–1953) and British pilot Edward "Mick" Mannock (1887–1918) participated in seventy-five and seventy-three air battles, respectively; Mannock, too, lost his life in combat. The most famous American air ace was Eddie Rickenbacker (1890–1973), who shot down twenty-six enemy aircraft. Later, he became a noted airline and automotive executive. During the war, American engineers designed pilotless, bomb-carrying aircraft, but the war ended before they could be put into production. By war's end in 1918, an estimated two hundred thousand planes had been built worldwide. Most had been manufactured for military use.

With the coming of peace, passenger and mail delivery routes using air travel were established in the United States. Then, in 1919, John Alcock (1892–1919) and Arthur Whitten-Brown (1886–1948) completed the first nonstop flight across the Atlantic Ocean. They flew from Newfoundland, Canada, in a Vicker's Vimy-Rolls-Royce, a twin-engine plane, and landed in Ireland; their flight-time was fifteen hours, thirty-seven minutes. However, paralleling such achievements were air-related tragedies. Less than a year after earning her pilot's license, Harriet Quimby died in an aviation accident, as did John Alcock several months after flying across the Atlantic and Tony Jannus two years after piloting the first passenger airplane.

❖ ASTRONOMY: EXPLORING THE HEAVENS

In 1912, astronomer Henrietta Leavitt (1868–1921) discovered that the period of time it takes for a Cepheid (a class of stars that brighten and dim at regular intervals) to complete its bright-dim cycle is linked to the star's luminosity (the amount of light emitted by a star or group of stars). Two years later, Harlow Shapley (1885–1972) utilized Leavitt's research to figure the relationship between luminosity and the distance between Cepheid variable stars. Such insights allowed astronomers to calculate large distances between stars and understand the size of the universe. In fact, Leavitt's and Shapley's work resulted in the dubbing of Cepheid-class stars as "yardsticks of the universe."

During the decade, George Ellery Hale (1868–1938), a professor of astrophysics at the University of Chicago, became the guiding force behind the construction of the world's largest telescope: a 100-inch reflecting instrument located at the Mount Wilson Observatory in Pasadena, California. The telescope weighed nearly two hundred thousand pounds, and was mounted in a 100-foot-high dome that was 100 feet in diameter. It allowed astronomers to observe three million stars, as well as faint nebulae (large bodies of dust or gas in interstellar space).

Hale's telescope remained the largest in the world until 1948. His efforts to build it also served as an example of a successful union between industry and science. His enthusiasm for astronomy and ability to excite an interest in the subject among nonastronomers allowed him to entice wealthy businessmen, among them fabled steel tycoon and philanthropist Andrew Carnegie (1835–1919), to fund the project.

❖ ATOMIC PHYSICS: UNLOCKING THE ATOM'S SECRETS

Great strides in the area of atomic physics were made during the 1910s. At the time, physicists generally agreed that all matter was composed of molecules, and that molecules were believed to be composed of still smaller units called atoms. As research progressed, it was becoming clear that atoms were composed of even smaller parts. The manner in which those parts came together remained a mystery.

In 1911, Ernest Rutherford (1871–1937), a New Zealand-born scientist working in England, put forth a revolutionary theory on the composition of the atom. Over a period of five years, Rutherford conducted experiments in which he fired alpha particles (positively charged particles consisting of two protons and two neutrons) at various substances, including sheets of gold. He first presented his theory in a paper he delivered in Manchester, England, and later he explained his theory before American physicists at Princeton University's Physics Colloquium. Rutherford's experiments led him to conclude that the center of the atom was composed of protons (from the Greek word for "first") that were surrounded by electrons. He believed that the atom was "built up like a solar system on an extremely small scale. The positive electricity is concentrated into a very small nucleus, which takes the place of the sun, and the negative electrons revolve around this like planets. It seems probable that they are arranged in rings, like the rings of Saturn."

Danish physicist Niels Henrik David Bohr (1885–1962) employed Rutherford's theory to speculate that an atom consisted of a single electron orbiting around a central proton, or nucleus.

American Robert A. Millikan (1868–1953), another of the era's pioneering physicists, charted the course of water and oil droplets flying through the air in an attempt to find the absolute charge of the electron. Austrian physicist Victor Hess (1883–1964) believed that the Earth itself might be the source of radiation. In a series of experiments, he made ten balloon flights in which he employed an electroscope (an instrument used to detect an electric charge) in an attempt to measure levels of radiation emanating from the Earth. Hess discovered that the radiation affecting the balloons was coming not from Earth but from space. These rays were dubbed "cosmic rays." Finally, English scientist Frederick Soddy (1877–1956) showed how atoms of different atomic weights could act in chemically identical ways, and American Irving Langmuir (1881–1957) studied the structure of electronic charges around the atomic nucleus. Excitement over atomic theory electrified the international scientific community during the 1910s. Yet it would remain for those who followed to unlock more of the atom's secrets.

❖ THE AUTOMOBILE: THE MODEL T AND AN INNOVATIVE INDUSTRY

In 1910, 458,500 motor vehicles were registered in the United States, and automobile manufacturing was fast becoming one of the nation's

. . . .

It was not surprising that the one-millionth patent awarded by the U.S. Patent Office was for an automobile-related accessory: an improved automobile tire. As President William Howard Taft (1857–1930) noted in the August 1911 issue of *Scientific American* magazine, "It was fitting that this patent, in itself a monument to progress, should have been awarded to an improvement in the automobile, for there is probably no single recent invention which has done so much to mark American progress or to show the world the prosperity of the United States."

major industries. The Model T, the Ford Motor Company's mass-produced automobile, revolutionized the car industry during the decade. On New Year's Day, 1910, the company opened its huge Highland Park, Michigan, factory where the Model Ts would be churned out by the thousands.

With regard to automobile production, Henry Ford (1863–1947), who had established the Ford Motor Company in 1903, revolutionized the process in 1913 when he introduced the assembly line. As a result of the faster, more efficient work completed on the assembly line, Ford reduced the hours of work for his employees from ten to eight per day. Additionally, he increased wages to $5.00 per day for some workers, at a time when daily salaries in the industry averaged $2.50. So successful was Ford's assembly line production in its division of labor, delivery of components to workers on the line, and the "planned, orderly, and continuous progression of the commodity through the shop" that assembly line production process came to be known as "Fordism." The process came to symbolize U.S. technological and manufacturing efficiency. By December 1913, it had reduced assembly time of a Model T to two hours and forty minutes; the following year, the assembly time decreased to one and one-half hours. Even with the rise in wages, such efficiency allowed Ford to lower the price of a new Model T. In 1910, a Model T sold for $850. By 1916, the cost had been reduced to $345. Eleven years later, the purchase price was down to $290.

Despite the popularity and affordability of the Model T, Ford did not completely monopolize the American automobile industry. In 1916, when Ford produced nearly 735,000 cars, the Willys-Overland company marketed 140,000 autos, Buick produced 124,834 cars, while Dodge made 71,400. Scores of smaller companies also produced automobiles. By 1916, there were more than three million cars in the United States.

Many important improvements in automotive engineering occurred during the decade. The all-steel automobile body was introduced, and the front-mounted engine that drove the rear axle by means of a rotating shaft (rather than a chain, as in some early cars) became the industry standard. Perhaps the most significant innovation was the development of the electric starter, which meant that engines no longer had to be started by a manually operated cranking mechanism. This innovation, more than any other, made automobiles easier to operate.

In addition, steam-powered vehicles and electric cars contended for a share of the automobile market. Steam-powered cars ran more smoothly than those with gas engines and freed the driver and passengers from irritating vibrations and difficult, often jerky gear-changing procedures. However, these engines were difficult to start since the water essential to their operation had to be boiled until pressure within the system reached 180 to 200 pounds per square inch. One model came with lengthy instruction for starting, beginning with "head the car into the wind!" Steam-powered cars were as expensive as they were inconvenient. In 1918, the Stanley Steamer was selling for $2,750, while the Model T cost less than $400. Meanwhile, electric cars only could be used for short trips, because their batteries had to be constantly recharged. The typical 1914 electric car was run by forty cells. Its speed was controlled by a pedal that, when released, caused the car to speed up and, when pressed, stopped the vehicle. The Stanley Company continued to sell steam-powered cars until 1927. However, by the end of the 1910s, the difficulties associated with charging and recharging electric cars resulted in their demise.

While most deliveries still were made by horse-drawn vehicles, trucks were beginning to displace horses. The tractor-trailer, a truck with its cab and engine separated from the main cargo body, was invented in 1915. This new vehicle made it possible for a truck driver to drop off one trailer and pick up another without unloading cargo. Also during the decade, politicians and business leaders stressed the importance of building better roads and a hard-surface transcontinental highway. In 1913, the U.S. Congress established a committee to explore the essentials of road construction. Three years later, it passed legislation allocating federal money for road-building. President Woodrow Wilson (1856–1924) was determined to veto the bill, because he believed that such construction should be state-funded. On the day he was to deliver his veto, a German submarine that had eluded the Allied surfaced in the harbor at Baltimore. While it

OPPOSITE PAGE
More affordable automobiles and better roads made transportation more accessible to all Americans, but also led to traffic jams like this on Forty-Second Street in New York City.

caused no immediate military threat, the submarine's presence was disconcerting, and it caused Wilson to reconsider his position. He then signed the legislation, arguing that improved roads had become a matter of national defense.

❖ BIOLOGICAL SCIENCES AND PUBLIC HEALTH: GENES, GERMS, AND SAFER FOOD

The 1910s saw significant developments in the biological sciences. In 1911, biologist Thomas Hunt Morgan (1866–1945) published the first chromosome map. The diagram identified the location of five sex-linked genes from the salivary glands of the Drosophila (fruit fly), and characterized the genes as being arranged like beads on a necklace. By the end of the decade, almost two thousand genes were mapped by Morgan and his colleagues.

Louise Pearce (1885–1959), one of a growing number of outstanding women scientists, discovered a cure for sleeping sickness. Caused by a micro parasite (a very small organism living in or on another organism) carried by the tsetse fly, those stricken with the disease suffered from inflammation of the brain and experienced listlessness. Pearce determined that Salvarsan, a drug then used as a cure for syphilis, stopped the disease in laboratory animals.

The first modern electric refrigerators were introduced in the United States in 1912 with the marketing of the popular Kelvinator model. Refrigeration led to an important advance in the food industry when Clarence Birdseye (1886–1956) developed a technique for preserving foods by freezing. He used two processes: one centering around the vaporizing of ammonia and the other involving a cold calcium chlorate solution. Birdseye quick-froze fish, fruit, and vegetables in 1924. His efforts eventually resulted in the creation of the multimillion-dollar frozen food industry.

The passing of new laws and codes and the establishment of health-oriented organizations resulted in foods reaching the marketplace in more healthful, less harmful forms. For example, raw milk easily can become a carrier of bacteria. In 1914, New York City's sanitary code required all milk to be pasteurized (heated to 145 degrees Fahrenheit and then rapidly cooled, killing bacteria). The resulting reduction of illness in the city led to pasteurization becoming a common practice across the country. Additionally, Americans became increasingly dependent upon canned goods in their diet. Cans had proven to be an economical form in which to transport food over long distances; the founding of the National Canning Association (NCA) in 1913 led to the establishment of safe canning standards.

During the decade, scientists and government officials attempted to increase public awareness of the need for cleanliness in food preparation. They stressed that the spread of germs is linked directly to maintaining one's health. Because insects often are carriers of germs, efforts were made to eradicate such pests. In Cleveland, for example, a municipal "Battle Against the House-Fly" was waged between 1913 and 1915. Public health officials sought to "put Cleveland on the map as a fly-less city" by setting out poison traps, teaching farmers and grocers about insect-breeding

Clarence Birdseye developed a food preservation method that eventually resulted in the creation of the multimillion-dollar frozen food industry. *Courtesy of the Library of Congress.*

habits, and draining water from stagnant pools. An extensive newspaper campaign combined with the distribution of two hundred thousand fly-swatters to the city's schoolchildren to increase public awareness of the link between flies and disease.

❖ CHEMISTRY AND PHYSICS: SHAPING OUR MODERN WORLD

The 1910s saw the beginning of what was to become the modern age of plastics. At the dawn of the decade, chemists faced the difficult problem of removing chemical residue from their equipment. One chemist, Leo Hendrik Baekeland (1863–1944), a Belgian-born American, set out to invent a solvent that would complete the task. Because he did not have any chemical residue at hand, he set about creating some to experiment on by combining phenol and formaldehyde. When he attempted to dissolve the substance he created, no solvent worked. It then occurred to Baekeland that the substance he created might itself have useful applications, and he set out to make it harder and tougher. By placing it under suitable temperatures and pressures, he discovered that he could create a liquid that, when cooled, took the shape of its container. Furthermore, this substance, once it was set, would not soften under heat. The chemist named it Bakelite, after himself. Bakelite, the first modern plastic, was marketed in 1917.

In 1910, French chemist Georges Claude (1870–1960) demonstrated that electricity passed through neon (a colorless, odorless, primarily inert gas) produced light, a discovery that directly led to the advent of roadway and storefront signs that could be brightly lit at night. The following year, Dutch scientist H. Kamerlingh Onnes (1853–1926) discovered superconductivity (the total disappearance of electrical resistance in a substance at temperatures approaching absolute zero). In 1912, German physicist Max von Laue (1879–1960) demonstrated that X rays scattered when passed through crystal structures; additionally, the patterns created could be identified on photographic plates. English physicists William Henry Bragg (1862–1942) and his son William Lawrence Bragg (1890–1971) successfully argued that these patterns could be used to identify the precise location of atoms in the crystal. In 1917, French physicist Paul Langevin (1872–1946) revolutionized oceanography (the science that focuses on the oceans) by inventing sonar (a mechanism that detects the presence and location of submerged objects via ultrasonic sound waves). The uses of all these inventions and discoveries were far-reaching. For example, in peacetime, sonar was used to detect schools of fish. In wartime, it was used to note the presence of enemy submarines.

❖ FREUDIAN THEORY: EXPLORING THE WORKINGS OF THE MIND

In 1909, Austrian neurologist and psychiatrist Sigmund Freud (1856–1939) traveled to the United States and delivered a series of five lectures at Clark University in Worcester, Massachusetts. These lectures stimulated interest in psychoanalysis in America. Freud already had devised practically all of the basic concepts of psychoanalysis. Among them are the concept that repressed thoughts, hidden away in an individual's unconscious, influence one's conscious action, and the understanding that experiences and relationships from one's past affect present-day relationships.

The following year, the International Association of Psychoanalysis was founded. By 1914, psychoanalytic societies existed in the United States, Germany, England, and Switzerland. Furthermore, the need to treat soldiers suffering from shell shock (a mental disturbance resulting from the stresses of combat) and civilians suffering traumas from their experiences in World War I (1914–18) further spurred an interest in Freudian analysis as well as in other schools of psychology.

❖ GEOLOGY: EXPLORING THE EARTH'S ORIGINS

In 1908, American geologist Frank Bursley Taylor (1860–1938) first put forth the theory of continental drift, which speculated that all the land on Earth originally had comprised a single, vast land mass. Four years later, German geologist, meteorologist, and explorer Alfred L. Wegener (1880–1930) proposed that this theory was the case approximately two hundred million years before. Wegener called this land mass *pangaea* (Greek for "all-Earth"). He argued that the planet's crust floated on a layer of basalt (a rock type), and that during the course of millions of years the original single supercontinent had broken up into the seven existing continents. He demonstrated that mountain chains on separate continents were composed of similar rock, and cited as evidence the unusual presence of coal deposits in Antarctica and glacial features in the topography of land near the equator. His detailed studies showed that the west coast of North America was moving six feet each year, and that during the previous hundred years Greenland had moved a mile farther away from Europe. Wegener's theory set off a scientific debate that raged for many years.

One other major geological theory was put forth during the decade. In 1914, German-born American geologist Beno Gutenberg (1889–1960) theorized that the Earth's core is liquid. He based his conclusion on his study of the nature of earthquakes.

❖ RADIO: REVOLUTIONIZING MEDIA

The early pioneers of radio included James Clerk Maxwell (1831–1879), a British theoretical physicist who in the 1860s speculated on the existence of radio waves; Heinrich R. Hertz (1857–1894), a German physicist who produced them experimentally in 1887; and Guglielmo

Marconi (1874–1937), an Italian inventor and physicist who in 1901 successfully received the initial transatlantic radio communication, sent from Cornwall in England to St. John's, Newfoundland.

The accomplishments of these men laid the groundwork for rapid advances in radio technology. Also in 1901, Reginald A. Fessenden (1866–1932) invented a high-frequency alternator (a device that produces alternating current) that manufactured a continuous radio wave. On Christmas Eve in 1906, Fessenden broadcast the first-ever voice radio transmission. Earlier that year, Lee De Forest (1873–1961) invented the triode, an electron tube with an anode (positive terminal), cathode (negative terminal), and a controlling grid. In 1912, Edwin H. Armstrong (1890–1954), a young electronics engineer, used the triode to create a "regenerative circuit," by which incoming radio signals could be amplified to such a degree that they could be played over speakers. During the following decade, Armstrong improved on this discovery. In 1918, he developed the superheterodyne radio receiver, which allowed for the reception of a wide range of radio transmissions. The following year, this receiver went into mass production.

During World War I, the U.S. government took control of radio technology. While doing so, the government provided funding to support additional technological developments and sorted out various patent infringements and controversies that had impeded the medium's evolution. (One of the most famous of these involved De Forest and Edwin H. Armstrong, with De Forest filing a lawsuit in which he claimed that he invented the regenerative circuit three years before Armstrong.) All of these inventions and events made possible the commercial radio industry, which entertained and enlightened masses of Americans beginning in the 1920s.

❖ SCIENCE ON THE FARM: FERTILIZERS AND OUTREACH

In 1910, farming was America's primary business. That year, more than one-fifth of the nation's population lived and worked on farms. During the decade, farm yields grew appreciably as a result of the application of scientific methods in all areas of farming.

The use of chemical fertilizers doubled between 1900 and 1910, and the growth of the fertilizer industry continued unabated during the following decade. Improvements in the quality and effectiveness of fertilizer, for example, the invention of a process by which atmospheric nitrogen was "fixed" into the substance, made high-quality chemical fertilizer more readily available and lower in cost.

The U.S. Department of Agriculture published and distributed to farmers millions of leaflets and short tracts covering a range of agricul-

The power and potential of radio was demonstrated on the night of April 14, 1912, during the sinking of the *Titanic*. The 882-foot-long White Star liner was then the world's largest ship and considered "unsinkable." This assumption provide false, however, when the ship sank on its maiden voyage from Southampton, England, to New York City. Among those drowned were 832 passengers and 685 crew members.

Radio first came into play when another ship signaled the *Titanic's* radio operator, informing him of the presence of icebergs in the new ship's path in the North Atlantic. The *Titanic*'s operator ignored these warnings, signaling back that he was busy with other matters. At 11:40 PM, the *Titanic* sideswiped an iceberg. Its starboard bow plates buckled under the impact, and the ship began to sink. As passengers scrambled aboard lifeboats, the previously lackadaisical radio operator employed the SOS (Save Our Ship) Morse Code signal to call for help. The radio operator on board the *Carpathia,* which was 58 miles away, picked up the signal, and the ship raced to the rescue. Three-and-a-half hours later, the *Carpathia* picked up 705 lifeboat survivors who otherwise faced certain death from exposure to the elements.

ture-related issues. These ranged from scientific advances in farming methods to newly available farming equipment.

❖ SOCIAL SCIENCE: THE RELATIONSHIP BETWEEN SCIENCE AND HUMANKIND

During the 1910s, advances in science and technology allowed many Americans to believe that scientific methods could improve governments, societies, and the general quality of life. John B. Watson (1878–1958), a behavioral psychologist, theorized that man had the ability to control human behavior. *The Principles of Scientific Management* (1911), authored by mechanical engineer Frederick Winslow Taylor (1856–1915), proposed new routines to increase worker efficiency and industrial productivity. In *The Place of Science in Modern Civilization* (1919) and *The Engineers and the Price System* (1921), sociologist Thorstein B. Veblen (1857–1929) suggested that America's engineers and technicians could shape "an effectual revolutionary overturn in America," resulting in the achievement of measurable social progress.

At the time, the theory of evolution originated by Charles Darwin (1809–1882) was increasingly churning up vigorous debate within the scientific community and society at large. Darwin postulated that species were capable of variations, and those in ecologically favorable environments would form new and distinct species. This concept clashed with those who placed the origins of mankind in the hands of a supernatural deity. Another of the decade's controversies involved eugenics, a movement that held that intelligence, like other human traits (such as hair color), is passed on from parent to child through the genes. Edward Lee Thorndike (1874–1949), a psychologist and educator, argued that intellectual differences "are due in large measure to original, inborn characteristics." He added that "we already know enough to justify us in providing for the original intellect and character of man in the future with a higher, purer source than the muddy streams of the past." Some eugenics supporters put forth a bold, highly controversial notion: criminality, imbecility, and laziness are inheritable traits, and those who demonstrated these traits should be discouraged, and even prohibited, from reproducing.

The U.S. Public Health Service at Ellis Island, New York, the main receiving point for those wishing to enter the country, sorted out immigrants "who may, because of their mental make-up, become a burden to the State or who may produce offspring that will require care in prisons, asylums, or other institutions." Such "mental defectives" were often refused entry into the United States.

❖ THE TECHNOLOGY OF WAR: SCIENCE AND SLAUGHTER

World War I was the single most significant world event of the 1910s. The emerging technology that allowed individuals to live more comfortably also was employed for the purposes of waging war, with terrible consequences.

Many European and American scientists and engineers served in the war effort. The machine gun, invented in the mid-nineteenth century and refined during the 1880s, became one of the deadliest weapons used in the war. A lightweight machine gun was developed, which was a significant improvement over those in use. Tanks were developed in England with the support of Winston Churchill (1874–1965), the British statesman who was then a military leader. They were first deployed at the Battle of the Somme in September 1916. Incendiary bombs and flamethrowers were invented or improved upon. Astronomer Forest Ray Moulton (1872–

1952) designed a more aerodynamic artillery shell to improve bombing. U.S. submarines were equipped with electric engines that allowed them to remain submerged longer than German U-boats. Utilizing radio technology, scientists William D. Coolidge (1873–1975) and Max Mason (1877–1961) developed long-range and short-range listening devices that helped to fix the distances that enemy guns could shoot. Naval engineers concocted an improved sea mine. In 1917, the U.S. Army had only fifty-five airplanes and thirty-five pilots; by the war's end, the military had forty-five squadrons of planes and more than seven hundred pilots. All of these technologies were used to improve the efficiency of killing.

In Nashville, Tennessee, the world's largest explosives factory churned out more than one hundred thousand pounds of explosive powder daily. For much of the war, mustard gas (a greenish-yellow poisonous gas with a pungent odor) was the chemical weapon of choice. The gas would stay suspended just above the ground, sink into the trenches, and torment victims through the agonizing process of burning the mucous membranes in their lungs and eyes until they collapsed and died. Though the Germans had initiated the use of poison gas in 1915, the Allies quickly followed suit. By the end of the war, American chemists had experimented with more than two dozen deadly gases for destructive use in the war.

For More Information

. . . .

BOOKS

Barr, Roger. *Radio: Wireless Sound.* San Diego: Lucent Books, 1994.

Bernstein, Jeremy. *Albert Einstein and the Frontiers of Physics.* New York: Oxford University Press, 1996.

Bunting, Eve. *SOS Titanic.* San Diego: Harcourt Brace, 1996.

Dolan, Terrance. *Probing Deep Space.* New York: Chelsea House, 1993.

Dowswell, Paul. *Weapons and Technology of World War I.* Chicago: Heinemann Library, 2002.

Fox, Karen. *The Chain Reaction: Pioneers of Nuclear Science.* New York: Franklin Watts, 1998.

Goldenstern, Joyce. *Albert Einstein: Physicist and Genius.* Springfield, NJ: Enslow Publishers, 1995.

Macdonald, Fiona. *The World in the Time of Albert Einstein.* Parsippany, NJ: Dillon Press, 1998.

Matthews, Tom L. *Always Inventing: A Photobiography of Alexander Graham Bell.* Washington, DC: National Geographic Society, 1999.

Maurer, Richard. *Rocket! How a Toy Launched the Space Age.* New York: Crown Publishers, 1995.

McCarthy, Pat. *Henry Ford: Building Cars for Everyone.* Berkeley Heights, NJ: Enslow Publishers, 2002.

Muckenhoupt, Margaret. *Sigmund Freud: Explorer of the Unconscious.* New York: Oxford University Press, 1997.

Pasachoff, Naomi. *Alexander Graham Bell: Making Connections.* New York: Oxford University Press, 1996.

Pringle, Laurence P. *Chemical and Biological Warfare: The Cruelest Weapons.* Berkeley Heights, NJ: Enslow Publishers, 2000.

Reef, Catherine. *Sigmund Freud: Pioneer of the Mind.* New York: Clarion Books, 2001.

Severance, John B. *Einstein: Visionary Scientist.* New York: Clarion Books, 1999.

Sommerville, Donald. *World War I.* Austin, TX: Raintree/Steck Vaughn, 1999.

Stewart, Gail B. *Weapons of War.* San Diego: Lucent Books, 2001.

Weitzman, David. *Model T: How Henry Ford Built a Legend.* New York: Crown Publishers, 2002.

WEB SITES

Person of the Century: Albert Einstein. http://www.time.com/time/time100/poc/home.html (accessed on August 2, 2002).

Robert Goddard. http://www.time.com/time/time100/scientist/profile/goddard.html (accessed on August 2, 2002).

Nobel e-Museum. Irving Langmuir-Biography. http://www.nobel.se/chemistry/laureates/1932/langmuir-bio.html (accessed on August 2, 2002).

Nobel e-Museum. Theodore William Richards. http://www.nobel.se/chemistry/laureates/1914/richards-bio.html (accessed on August 2, 2002).

chapter eight *Sports*

1910: **April** William Howard Taft becomes the first U.S. president to inaugurate the baseball season by throwing out the first ball.

1910: **July 4** Jack Johnson retains his heavyweight boxing crown by pummeling James J. Jeffries in a fifteen-round bout.

1911: **May 30** Ray Harroun wins the first-ever Indianapolis 500 auto race.

1912: The earned run average (which measures a pitcher's success) becomes a recognized baseball statistic in the National League (NL); the American League (AL) follows suit the following season.

1912: **April 12** The famed Tinker-to-Evers-to-Chance double play combination appears in its last game together for the Chicago Cubs.

1912: **April 20** Fenway Park, home of baseball's Boston Red Sox, opens.

1912: **May 5–July 22** The fifth Olympic Games are held in Stockholm, Sweden.

1913: Baseball's major-league New York Highlanders are rechristened the Yankees.

1913: **February 5** The New York State Athletic Commission votes unanimously to prohibit interracial boxing competition.

1913: **March 8** In baseball, the upstart Federal League is organized to challenge the American and National Leagues.

1913: **April 5** Brooklyn's major league baseball team plays its first game in Ebbets Field, an exhibition against the New York Yankees.

1913: **July 25–28** The United States wins its first Davis Cup tennis championship since 1902, defeating Great Britain three matches to two.

1914: **April 22** Nineteen-year-old Babe Ruth makes his professional baseball debut with the International League's Baltimore team. He pitches a shutout victory over Buffalo.

1914: **July 4** In the first-ever victory by an American crew, eight Harvard men win the Grand Challenge Cup at the Henley Royal Regatta in England.

1914: **July 11** Babe Ruth makes his major league debut as a pitcher with the Boston Red Sox, earning a 4 to 3 victory over the Cleveland Indians.

1914: **September 29** The "Miracle" Boston Braves, in last place as recently as mid-July, clinch the National League pennant.

1915: **April 5** Jess Willard knocks out Jack Johnson in the twenty-sixth round and becomes heavyweight champ.

1915: **August 18** Braves Field, new home of the Boston Braves, opens.

1915: **October 9** Woodrow Wilson becomes the first U.S. president to attend a World Series game.

1916: **February 7** An organizing committee establishes the Professional Golfers' Association (PGA).

1916: **February 7** A Federal League lawsuit charging the rival American and National Leagues with antitrust violations is dismissed in U.S. District Court by Judge Kenesaw M. Landis, future baseball commissioner.

1916: **April 1** The Amateur Athletic Union (AAU) holds the initial women's indoor and outdoor national swimming championships.

1916: **April 10** The first-ever PGA golf tournament is held.

1916: **October 7** In the most lopsided victory in college football history, Georgia Tech beats Cumberland College 222 to 0.

1917: **June 1** Boston Braves catcher Hank Gowdy becomes the first major league ballplayer to enlist in the military during World War I.

1917: **October 26** St. Louis Cardinals manager Miller Huggins is signed to manage the New York Yankees.

1918: **August 2** Because of World War I, the U.S. government orders major league baseball to end its season on September 1 but permits the World Series to be played.

1919: Sir Barton becomes the first racehorse to win the Triple Crown.

1919: **August 13** Man o' War suffers the lone defeat in the horse's career, losing to a horse named Upset at the Sanford Stakes in Saratoga, New York.

1919: **April 19** New York Governor Al Smith signs a bill legalizing Sunday baseball in the state.

1919: **July 4** Jack Dempsey knocks out Jess Willard in the third round to become heavyweight boxing champ.

1919: **October** Several members of the Chicago White Sox throw (intentionally lose) the World Series.

1919: **December 26** The New York Yankees purchase Babe Ruth from Boston Red Sox owner Harry Frazee.

Overview

In the sports world, the 1910s was a decade of firsts. The initial Indianapolis 500 auto race was held. The Professional Golfers' Association (PGA) was established. Records were smothered at the 1912 Olympic Games in Stockholm, Sweden, and women's competitions were added. Sir Barton won horse racing's first Triple Crown.

In the 1910s, basketball still was in its infancy, having only been invented in 1891. It was primarily a college competition. The few professional leagues that existed were poorly run and doomed to failure. However, several individual pro teams won fame, including the Buffalo Germans and original Celtics. They took on all opponents, rather than playing in leagues. The Celtics were formed in New York and should not be confused with the present-day Boston Celtics. In particular, they were a major influence in the development of the sport.

Football, like basketball, mostly was played in college. While individual universities from across the country fielded exceptional teams, the game was dominated by Ivy League teams. Before the decade began, football was a notoriously violent activity. Players at the college level frequently were injured and some even died. During the decade, groundbreaking rules were employed to ease the sport's violence.

The era's dominant boxer, Jack Johnson, was as controversial as he was talented. Johnson, the heavyweight champion between 1908 and 1915, was an African American. He was resented by the masses not only because of his skin color, but because he refused to act in a subservient manner. As Johnson pummeled various "great white hopes" in the ring, he was a source of inspiration to those of his race. (The term "great white hope" was later used to refer to any white athlete whom white audiences hoped would dethrone a black champion.)

If boxers usually were the sons of immigrants and the products of poverty, those who participated in golf and tennis were at the opposite end of the economic and social scale. In golf, the social barriers began to be torn down by two daring, talented players. One, Francis Ouimet, was an amateur. The other, Walter Hagen, was a professional. Meanwhile, during the decade, middle-class Americans increasingly began taking up tennis, which was one of the few sports in which women competed as successfully as men.

The modern-era Olympic Games were first held in 1896. The 1910s saw only one competition, in 1912, and it was marred by controversy. At those games, Jim Thorpe earned two gold medals in the grueling decathlon and pentathlon competition. Soon afterward, he was stripped of both by the International Olympic Committee (IOC) because he had briefly played semiprofessional baseball prior to competing in the Olympics. The medals were returned to his family in 1982, however, almost three decades after Thorpe's death.

In baseball, the decade saw its share of thrilling games during the regular season and in the World Series. The Philadelphia Athletics and Boston Red Sox were the dominating teams, respectively winning three and four World Series. The Federal League briefly challenged the established American and National Leagues for domination in the sport. Not only did the Federal League set up teams and begin play, they attempted to lure away some of the top major league stars. After a couple of years of friction, the Federal League folded. However, an even more ominous threat to the national pastime came at the end of the decade, when eight Chicago White Sox ballplayers accepted, or knew of, bribes to throw the 1919 World Series. At the beginning of the following decade, the scandal threatened to destroy the integrity of the game.

A host of hall-of-fame ballplayers began their careers or starred during the decade. A short list includes Ty Cobb, Walter Johnson, Honus Wagner, Tris Speaker, Eddie Collins, and the ill-fated "Shoeless" Joe Jackson (who would be implicated in what came to be known as the Black Sox scandal). Perhaps the most celebrated of all major leaguers debuted during the 1910s: a young Boston Red Sox pitcher named Babe Ruth. During the last week of the decade, Ruth was sold to the New York Yankees, a team that, at the time, had neither appeared in nor won a World Series. Not only would this transaction result in the transformation of the Yankees into a dominating force in baseball, but Ruth's ball field heroics (in the batter's box, rather than on the pitching mound) would save the sport from the spectre of scandal.

Ty Cobb (1886–1961) Ty Cobb, the "Georgia Peach," was one of the all-time great baseball players. His lifetime batting average (.366) is the highest in major league history. At the end of the twentieth century, he was second all-time in hits (4,189), first in runs scored (2,245), and fourth in steals (892). With one exception, Cobb was the American League batting champion each year throughout the 1910s. In 1936, he became the first ballplayer elected to the Baseball Hall of Fame. However, Cobb was not the world's most beloved human being. He was reportedly mean-tempered and egocentric, a tyrant and a racist. Upon his death, only three baseball professionals attended his funeral. *Photo reproduced by permission of Archive Photos, Inc.*

"Shoeless" Joe Jackson (1889–1951) If not for his involvement, however great or small, in the 1919 Black Sox scandal, "Shoeless" Joe Jackson undoubtedly would be enshrined in the Baseball Hall of Fame. In his thirteen-year major league career he batted .356. During 1911, his first full season, he hit .408. The following year, his average slipped to .395. Babe Ruth even was known to have copied his swing. During 1920, his final season, Jackson hit .382. He was just thirty-one years old, yet his career was over. He and seven of his Chicago White Sox teammates were banned from baseball for life for throwing the 1919 World Series.

Jack Johnson (1878–1946) Decades before the rise of Muhammad Ali (1941–), an African American heavyweight champ who shocked mainstream sensibilities, Jack Johnson ruled the boxing world and similarly angered the white majority. During the 1910s and for decades to come, African Americans were expected to accept their status as second-class citizens. Johnson refused to do so. He lived a flamboyant lifestyle and defeated all "great white hope" comers. Johnson fled the country in 1912 after being convicted of violating the Mann Act and lost his title three years later in a match in Cuba. He returned to the U.S. in 1920, was sentenced to a year in jail, and eventually drifted into obscurity. *Photo reproduced by permission of AP/Wide World Photos.*

Walter Johnson (1887–1946) Walter Johnson was one of the greatest pitchers ever to wear a baseball uniform. From 1907 to 1927, he pitched exclusively for the Washington Senators, winning an astounding 417 major league games. This is the second-most in history, behind Cy Young (1867–1955). Johnson won twenty or more games each season from 1910 through 1919; in 1912 and 1913, he totaled thirty-three and thirty-six victories. Yet amazingly, for almost half his career, he pitched for second-division teams. Additionally, for decades, Johnson held the all-time strike-out mark (3,506). His career ERA was 2.17, and he threw a record 110 shut-outs. *Photo reproduced by permission of AP/Wide World Photos.*

John McGraw (1873–1934) After starring at third base for the Baltimore Orioles during the 1890s, John McGraw became manager of the New York Giants in 1904. For the next three decades, he was one of baseball's most dominating skippers and most colorful, celebrated personalities. His teams earned ten pennants, winning four straight from 1921 to 1924. McGraw was famed for being a brilliant strategist and tough competitor who dominated his players; it was for good reason that he earned the nickname "Little Napoleon." He also was one of the first managers to acknowledge the value of relief pitching. *Photo reproduced by permission of AP/Wide World Photos.*

Francis Ouimet (1893–1967) Today, Francis Ouimet is not as well-remembered as other celebrated golfers, from Bobby Jones and Ben Hogan to Arnold Palmer and Jack Nicklaus. However, during the 1910s, Ouimet was responsible for popularizing the game. He accomplished this by winning the U.S. Open title in 1913, despite his working-class background. Ouimet, who was employed as a stockbroker, remained an amateur for the rest of his athletic career. In 1951, he became the first non-British citizen elected captain of the Royal and Ancient Golf Club of St. Andrews in Scotland. *Photo reproduced by permission of the Corbis Corporation.*

Jim Thorpe (1888–1953) Jim Thorpe was a Renaissance man among athletes. He first earned fame playing football for coach Glenn "Pop" Warner (1871–1954) at the Carlyle Indian School. At the 1912 Olympics, he won gold medals in the decathlon and pentathlon. He played major league baseball from 1913 to 1919 and professional football between 1915 and 1928. He was inducted into the Pro Football Hall of Fame in 1953. In 1950, the Associated Press (AP) named Thorpe the top athlete of the first half of the twentieth century. *Photo reproduced by permission of AP/Wide World Photos.*

◆◆◆ *Topics in the News*

❖ AUTO RACING: THE INDIANAPOLIS 500

The first Indianapolis 500 auto race was held on Memorial Day, 1911, at the Indianapolis Motor Speedway. Back then, the race was known as the International Sweepstakes; as today, it consisted of 200 laps around the speedway's two-and-one-half-mile, oval-shaped track.

That first year, Ray Harroun (1879–1968) was the victor. His car, a yellow and black six-cylinder Marmon, averaged what then was an incredible speed: 74.602 miles per hour. For his victory, Harroun won a $10,000 prize. (By the 1990s, drivers regularly topped more than 200 miles per hour and emerged with million-dollar purses.) His car reportedly was the initial single-seat racecar, and the first to be equipped with a rearview mirror.

Early on, the Indy 500 featured thrilling finishes. A typical one occurred in 1915. For much of the race, Ralph DePalma (1883–1956) and Dario Resta (1882 or 1884–1924) jockeyed for the lead. DePalma's Mercedes gave way on lap 197, but he was able to crawl around the track on the car's three remaining operable cylinders and still finish less than four minutes ahead of Resta. (Three years earlier, DePalma was not as fortunate. He led from lap 3 to 198, at which point his Mercedes sputtered and died. He and his mechanic pushed the car over a mile to the pits, but by then the race was over.)

The 1916 race was shortened to 300 miles because of the war in Europe. It had the smallest field of contestants and the fewest spectators of any Indy 500. This time, Resta dominated and won. After a two-year hiatus caused by the war, the race resumed in 1919. For the first time, qualifying speeds broke 100 miles per hour. The winner, Howard "Howdy" Wilcox (c. 1889–1923), cruised to victory, averaging just over 88 miles per hour. However, most of the cars in the race either crashed or broke down. The race also saw its first fatalities, as three were killed and two were seriously injured.

Although he won just once at Indianapolis during the 1910s, Ralph DePalma was considered the era's top driver. In the seven Indy 500s in which he competed, he led for 613 out of 1,400 laps. At the end of the decade, he held the world land-speed record of 149 miles per hour.

❖ BASEBALL'S TUMULTUOUS DECADE

In baseball, the 1910s was a decade of milestones and classic major league contests, a challenge from an upstart league, and a dark, looming

Indianapolis 500 Winners

Year	Driver
1911	Ray Harroun
1912	Joe Dawson
1913	Jules Goux
1914	Rene Thomas
1915	Ralph DePalma
1916	Dario Resta
1917	(not held)
1918	(not held)
1919	Howard "Howdy" Wilcox

scandal. The year 1910 itself was full of milestones: William Howard Taft (1857–1930) became the first U.S. president to throw out the first ball at an opening-day game. Pitcher Cy Young (1867–1955) earned his five-hundredth major league victory. In one memorable early August contest, Philadelphia Athletics and Chicago White Sox pitchers Jack Coombs (1882–1957) and Ed Walsh (1881–1959) battled each other for sixteen innings, with the game ending in a 0 to 0 tie. Several days later, a game between the Pittsburgh Pirates and Brooklyn Superbas (Dodgers) featured the most unusual box score in major league history. Each team had eight runs and thirteen hits in thirty-eight at-bats, three walks, five strike-outs, one hit-batsman, one passed ball, thirteen assists, and two errors. (One other regular-season game that rivaled these two came in May 1917, when Chicago Cubs and Cincinnati Reds hurlers Hippo Vaughn [1888–1966] and Fred Toney [1888–1953] each pitched nine-inning no-hitters!) Finally, Ty Cobb (1886–1961) nipped Napoleon Lajoie (1874–1959) for the American League batting championship; their averages were .3850687 and .3840947.

The American and National Leagues were firmly entrenched as the nation's leading baseball organizations. However, in 1913, the Federal League was formed. It was well funded and organized, and it commenced play in May. The league also began raiding the majors for players. That November, St. Louis Browns player-manager George Stovall (1878–1951) became the first major leaguer to jump to the Federal League. Many established players

World Series Champions

Year	Winning Team (League)	Losing Team (League)
1910	Philadelphia Athletics (AL) 4	Chicago Cubs (NL) 1
1911	Philadelphia Athletics (AL) 4	New York Giants (NL) 2
1912	Boston Red Sox (AL) 4	New York Giants (NL) 3
1913	Philadelphia Athletics (AL) 4	New York Giants (NL) 1
1914	Boston Braves (NL) 4	Philadelphia Athletics (AL) 0
1915	Boston Red Sox (AL) 4	Philadelphia Phillies (NL) 1
1916	Boston Red Sox (AL) 4	Brooklyn Dodgers (NL) 1
1917	Chicago White Sox (AL) 4	New York Giants (NL) 2
1918	Boston Red Sox (AL) 4	Chicago Cubs (NL) 2
1919	Cincinnati Reds (NL) 5	Chicago White Sox (AL) 3

were offered contracts, and a few even signed with the upstart league. After two years of friction and lawsuits, however, the Federal League folded.

Not all threats to the game were external. In May 1912, fiery Ty Cobb (1886–1961) charged into the stands and attacked a heckler. A fight between fans and Cobb's Detroit teammates followed, and American League President Ban Johnson (1864–1931) suspended Cobb indefinitely. In response, the players went on strike. In order to avoid a $5,000 fine for failing to field a team, Tigers owner Frank Navin (1871–1935) recruited local amateurs for the team's next game, which the Tigers lost to the Philadelphia Athletics, 24 to 2. Two days later, the real Tigers resumed play.

The decade ended with one of the game's darkest incidents. The Chicago White Sox, the World Series winners in 1917, were favored to beat their opponents, the Cincinnati Reds, in the 1919 fall classic. However, the Reds won and, during the last month of the 1920 season, it was learned that certain members of the Sox accepted, or had knowledge of, bribes from gamblers to throw the series. Eventually, eight players were banned from baseball for life: outfielders Happy Felsch and "Shoeless" Joe Jackson; third-baseman Buck Weaver; shortstop Swede Risberg; first-baseman Chick Gandil; pitchers Eddie Cicotte and Claude Williams; and utility infielder Fred McMullen.

Babe Ruth was a stellar pitcher for the Boston Red Sox and home-run hitter for the New York Yankees. Courtesy of the Library of Congress.

❖ WORLD SERIES THRILLS

During the 1910s, two ball clubs dominated major league baseball. The Philadelphia Athletics won the World Series three times, in 1910, 1911, and 1913. The team, which in 1954 moved to Kansas City and fourteen years later became the Oakland A's, was owned and managed by Connie Mack (1862–1956). When Mack retired in 1950, at age eighty-seven, he had managed the team for a half-century, which was a record for longevity that likely never will be broken. Among the team's stars during the 1910s were pitchers Jack Coombs, Chief Bender, and Eddie Plank, second-baseman Eddie Collins, and third baseman Frank "Home Run" Baker. Collins, Baker, shortstop Jack Barry, and first baseman Stuffy McInnis came to be known as Mack's "$100,000 infield." After losing the 1914 World Series to the Boston Braves, Mack began dismantling his team. He released some of his players and sold others to other ball clubs. Reportedly, Mack did so to raise needed funds; however, his decision to release some of his players suggests that he believed they might have thrown the Series.

The Boston Red Sox were World Series champs four times, in 1912, 1915, 1916, and 1918. Among the baseball greats who played on one or more Red Sox teams were pitchers "Smokey" Joe Wood, Dutch Leonard, Ernie Shore, and Babe Ruth; shortstop Honus Wagner; and outfielders Tris Speaker,

Harry Hooper, and Duffy Lewis. The 1912 World Series, in which the Sox bested the New York Giants four games to three, was particularly exciting. Four games were decided by one run; a fifth ended in an eleven-inning tie. Spectacular catches warded off near-defeat. In the climactic game, the Sox scored twice in the bottom of the tenth inning to take the Series.

The 1915 series was noted for the first postseason appearance by a legend-to-be: Babe Ruth (1895–1948), who briefly played for the Sox during the previous season and now was in the majors to stay. He appeared in one game, as an unsuccessful pinch hitter. Before becoming a home-run-hitting legend for the New York Yankees in the 1920s, Ruth enjoyed a solid, Hall-of-Fame caliber career as a Red Sox pitcher. In the 1916 and 1918 World Series, Ruth pitched twenty-nine and two-thirds consecutive scoreless innings. However, just after Christmas 1919, Red Sox owner Harry Frazee (1881–1929) sold the ballplayer to the New York Yankees for $100,000 and a $300,000 loan. While Ruth went on to become the "Sultan of Swat" and lead the Yankees to glory, the Red Sox never won another World Series during the twentieth century.

In 1914, another Boston team won the World Series: the Boston Braves (who moved to Milwaukee in the 1950s and became the Atlanta Braves in the 1960s). As late as July 19, the Braves were languishing in the National League cellar. However, a late-season drive allowed the Braves to creep up in the standings and move into first place. Then, in the World Series, the "Miracle Braves" beat the Athletics in four straight games. It was the first World Series sweep in major league history.

❖ BASKETBALL ENDURES GROWING PAINS

During the 1910s, basketball primarily was a college sport. It became so after James Naismith (1861–1939), a Young Men's Christian Association (YMCA) Training School instructor, invented the game in 1891. By 1910, regional conferences had been established, consisting of area schools. The powerhouse teams included those from Indiana's Wabash College, which between 1908 and 1911 compiled a 66 and 3 record, and Wisconsin, which won or shared the Western Conference title from 1912 to 1914 and again in 1916 and 1918.

During the early twentieth century, attempts to establish professional basketball leagues met with failure. They were poorly organized; often during the same season, players switched teams and leagues. The era's most successful noncollegiate teams were those that remained outside of any league and instead traveled about, or barnstormed, taking on all challengers. One such team was the Buffalo Germans, which started out as a YMCA club. After demonstrating basketball techniques at the 1904

Olympics, the team turned professional. Between 1895 and 1925, the Germans compiled a 792 and 86 record. The era's other notable teams included the New York Whirlwinds, arguably the top squad during the first part of the decade, and the Philadelphia SPHAs (named for the

The Great White Hope

Jack Johnson's career in and out of the ring was recounted loosely decades later in *The Great White Hope,* a Pulitzer Prize-winning play written by Howard Sackler (1929–1982). While his name was changed to "Jack Jefferson," the major events of his life were portrayed. Sackler's depiction of the prevailing racial attitudes of the 1910s resonated with 1960s audiences, who were grappling with the consequences of the Civil Rights movement.

The Great White Hope premiered at Washington D.C.'s Arena Stage in 1967. The following year it came to Broadway's Alvin Theatre, where it ran for 556 performances. Then in 1970, it was made into a motion picture. James Earl Jones (1931–) played Jefferson in all three productions.

South Philadelphia Hebrew Association), an all-Jewish team that began play in 1918.

The decade also saw the emergence of the major pioneering professional team: the original Celtics (not to be confused with the present-day Boston Celtics), which were organized in New York in 1918. The Celtics most often played amateur and local teams, and won more than 90 percent of its games. Their roster included such early century legends as Nat Holman, Joe Lapchick, Swede Grimstead, Johnny Beckman, Chris Leonard, and Henry "Dutch" Dehnert. All were signed to the first individual contracts in basketball history and were paid by the season rather than by the game. This not only ended the practice of players haphazardly switching teams or leagues but resulted in the evolution of team strategies. The Celtics constantly experimented both individually and as a team and developed such tactics as the pivot play, switching defense, and give-and-go offense.

❖ BOXING'S CONTROVERSIAL CHAMP

The 1910s began with one of the twentieth century's most memorable heavyweight championship bouts. Since 1908, Jack Johnson (1878–1946) had been champ. Johnson was unpopular with the masses not only because he was an African American, but also because he openly delighted in his celebrity and refused to act humbly, as was expected of those of his race. Because Johnson was pounding all challengers, James J. Jeffries (1875– 1953), a beloved former champ, was coaxed out of retirement to face him. Even though Jeffries was out of shape, it was expected that he easily would emerge victorious. This did not happen, though. The two met in July 1910, in Reno, Nevada, with Johnson dominating the fifteen-round match and retaining the title. In response, race riots broke out in cities across the country. Groups of whites attacked and beat innocent black Americans, reminding them that even though a black man had just pummeled a white man in an athletic competition, many whites were willing to use force to make sure that blacks knew they still were considered second-class citizens.

Eventually, the government accomplished what no boxer could. In 1912, Johnson was convicted of violating the Mann Act, a federal law that forbade individuals from transporting women across state lines for "immoral purposes," such as prostitution. Before he could be jailed, Johnson left the country. He did not return until 1920.

Johnson still retained his title, which he lost three years later in another fabled championship bout. Jess Willard (1881–1968), a six-foot-seven-inch Kansan, knocked out a rusty, out-of-shape Johnson in the twenty-sixth round of a match staged in Havana, Cuba. Johnson eventually alleged that he threw the fight for $50,000 and an exemption from his prison sentence. The decade ended with the rise of another all-time-great heavyweight: Jack Dempsey (1895–1983). By the third round of their 1919 encounter, Dempsey had so battered Willard that the champ did not come out for the fourth round. Dempsey remained heavyweight champion until 1926.

Because of its violent nature, even by the late 1910s boxing had gained only a limited measure of popularity and respectability in the United States. In fact, boxing matches remained barred in many states. However, the sport became more reputable with the rise of such popular champs as Dempsey. Additionally, during World War I (1914–18), the military employed the sport to train recruits. Afterward, states began repealing antiboxing legislation.

❖ THE BRUTAL GAME OF COLLEGE FOOTBALL

In the 1910s, football was wildly popular on university campuses. Students strongly related to their school's teams and each fall, thousands viewed games amid much celebration. However, during the previous decade, football had been a violent sport, so much so that eighteen college players were killed in games played during the 1905 season. It was hoped that the addition of new regulations would ease the brutality. A neutral zone was created between the offensive and defensive lines; the forward pass was legalized; and the yardage required for a first-down was increased from five to ten yards. However, between 1905 and 1910, 113 players still died while competing in the sport. Further changes were instituted in 1910: seven men now were required on the line of scrimmage; games were divided into four quarters, each lasting fifteen minutes; and such practices as the flying tackle, the interlocking of arms while running interference, and the pulling and pushing of the ball carrier to advance the pigskin were deemed illegal. Two years later, an end zone was created behind each goal post, the score of a touchdown was increased from five to six points, and teams were allowed four downs to attain a first down. As the decade progressed, improvements in such protective equipment as pads and helmets were introduced. All these changes altered the character of the game. While football still was no gentle pastime, the number of deaths and injuries markedly decreased.

During the decade, the powerhouse college football teams were found in the Ivy League, among such schools as Harvard, Princeton, and Yale. In fact, the 1910s was the final decade in which the Ivy League dominated the sport. Between 1908 and 1916, Harvard ran up a record of 71 and 7, with five ties. In 1912, the Crimson wrecked bids by Yale and Princeton for undefeated seasons.

Concurrently, other colleges began dominating the sport. In 1911 and 1912, Notre Dame, destined to field some of the century's top college football squads, completed undefeated seasons. In 1913, the team masterfully employed the forward pass. In a celebrated 35 to 13 victory against Army, Notre Dame quarterback Gus Dorais (1891–1954) completed thirteen of seventeen passes for 243 yards. Quite a few were caught by Knute Rockne (1888–1931), who before the decade ended was named the team's coach. Rockne was destined to become one of the century's college coaching legends.

Other powers also emerged. In the Midwest, Illinois, coached by the legendary Robert Zuppke (1879–1957), enjoyed an undefeated season in 1914, scoring 224 points while holding its opponents to just 22. Another undefeated season followed in 1915. Minnesota, Ohio State, and the University of Pittsburgh also had strong teams. In the South, Georgia Tech emerged as the region's top football program. In 1915, the school began a thirty-two-game winning streak that lasted for more than five seasons. In one of the most lopsided scores in college football history, Georgia Tech defeated Cumberland College, 222 to 0, in 1916. The team was coached by John Heisman (1869–1936), for whom the Heisman Trophy (awarded each year to the nation's top college football player) is named. In the West, the University of Washington dominated. The Huskies did not lose a game between 1908 and 1916.

Collegiate Football National Champions

Year	College
1910	Harvard
1911	Princeton
1912	Harvard
1913	Harvard
1914	Army
1915	Cornell
1916	University of Pittsburgh
1917	Georgia Tech
1918	University of Pittsburgh
1919	Georgia Tech

❖ THE UNSTABLE GAME OF PROFESSIONAL FOOTBALL

Before 1910, professional football mainly was a haphazard enterprise. There were no important professional leagues; many teams refused to form or enter leagues and regularly raided talent from college teams. During a season, players often jumped from team to team, most of which were clustered in Pennsylvania, Ohio, and in the Chicago, Illinois, area. Competition was uneven and gambling scandals were frequent.

However, a bit of stability did come to professional football during the 1910s. The main professional league was centered in Ohio, with the Canton Bulldogs, Columbus Panhandlers, Youngstown Patricians, and Dayton Triangles among the league's more colorfully named teams. The decade's one great professional football star was Jim Thorpe (1888–1953), who in 1912 scored 25 touchdowns and 190 points for his Carlyle Indian School football team. Thorpe signed with the Canton Bulldogs in 1915. His starting salary was $250 per game, an enormous sum for the era. During the 1916 season, Thorpe led his team to ten straight victories. The Bulldogs claimed the then-unofficial title of world champions that year, and did so again in 1917 and 1919.

❖ GOLF'S GROWING POPULARITY

During the first two decades of the twentieth century, the popularity of golf rapidly increased. However, at the time, the sport primarily was restrict-

U.S. Golf Association Open Champions

Year	Player
1910	Alex Smith
1911	John J. McDermott
1912	John J. McDermott
1913	Francis Ouimet
1914	Walter Hagen
1915	Jerome D. Travers
1916	Chick Evans
1917	(not played)
1918	(not played)
1919	Walter Hagen

ed to the upper classes. Golf was played on country club courses, by those of the "privileged" class. Unlike boxing, where champions often were uneducated street boys, golfers usually had well-to-do backgrounds. Golf was not so much a competitive sport as a "gentleman's game," played as a hobby.

However, during the 1910s, two outstanding golfers earned their first acclaim and broke down the game's social barriers. Walter Hagen (1892–1969), a professional who was to enjoy a long and successful career, won his first U.S. Open title in 1914. Back then, professional golfers were considered to be socially inferior to those players who did not accept financial compensation for competing in matches. Professionals received little money for their efforts; during open tournaments, they even were barred from clubhouses. However, Hagen, with his affable, confident personality, challenged this social discrimination by simply ignoring the rules. Pretending to be unaware of regulations barring professionals, he entered clubhouses and locker rooms during open competitions. Eventually, country clubs ceased enforcing such rules. Hagen's actions helped to transform golf into a respectable occupation. Before the decade ended, the Professional Golfer's Association (PGA) was established to foster interest in the game and increase the standard of living for professional golfers. In 1916, the first national PGA tournament was held at the Siwanoy Golf Course in Bronxville, New York.

OPPOSITE PAGE
Professional golfers (left to right) Johnny Parnell, Bobby Jones, Walter Hagen, and Gene Sarazen. Although professional golfers such as these began to break down the social barriers, the game continued to be played mainly by the upper class.
Reproduced by permission of AP/Wide World Photos.

Aside from Hagen, Francis Ouimet (1893–1967) was the era's most influential golfer. Ouimet was only twenty when he won the 1913 U.S. Open title in a three-way playoff. It was an upset victory, crammed with drama. Ouimet came from behind to tie two leading British-born professionals, Harry Vardon (1870–1937) and Edward "Ted" Ray (b. 1878). Then

Kentucky Derby Winners

Year	Horse
1910	Donau
1911	Meridian
1912	Worth
1913	Donerail
1914	Old Rosebud
1915	Regret
1916	George Smith
1917	Omar Khayyam
1918	Exterminator
1919	Sir Barton

he smothered them in a playoff, topping them by five and six strokes. What made Ouimet's accomplishment even more noteworthy was his working-class background. He had grown up in Brookline, Massachusetts, where his French-Canadian immigrant father toiled as a gardener. Ouimet and his brother became caddies at the upscale Brookline Country Club. Although caddies were not allowed to play on the club's course, the Ouimet boys often sneaked in practice strokes. Determined to enter the tournaments held at the club, Ouimet earned additional money by working in a dry-goods store. In 1909, while attending Brookline High School, he won Boston's interscholastic golf competition. Even though he failed to qualify for the U.S. Amateur Championship in 1910, 1911, and 1912, he lasted into the final rounds of the Massachusetts Amateur Championship in 1912. The following year, he won the title and qualified for the U.S. Open.

Ouimet was the first amateur to win the Open. Even more important-ly, his background was highly publicized, and his victory helped transform golf into a popular recreational activity to be enjoyed by people of all social classes. The following year, he became U.S. Amateur champion and won the French Amateur title.

❖ HORSE RACING

The 1910s saw the Kentucky Derby attain its status as the world's most celebrated horse race. The Derby had been running since 1875.

However, from 1899 through 1914, the major northeastern stables side-stepped the race, choosing instead to enter the American Derby in Chicago. The Kentucky race then became a low-profile, regional event. In 1915, Harry Payne Whitney (1872–1930), a famed horse breeder-financier, chose to participate. He entered Regret, a filly (a young female horse). Dispelling the notion that a three-year-old filly would be unable to beat a colt in a mile-and-a-quarter race, Regret led throughout and won. The subsequent publicity earned the Derby the stature it enjoys to this day.

Other important races during the period included the Saratoga Cup, the Belmont Stakes, the Alabama, the Champagne, the Preakness, and the Withers. If a horse went on to victory in the Kentucky Derby, Preakness, and Belmont Stakes, each of which was held in the spring, it won the Triple Crown, the most desirable and elusive prize in American thoroughbred horseracing. The decade saw one horse, Sir Barton, win the first-ever Triple Crown.

Meanwhile, during the decade, all of horse racing was threatened by a national reform movement to discourage gambling and betting. In New York, the sport was shut down for two years beginning in 1910, when bookmaking and gaming devices were prohibited under a new law, the Director's Liability Act. Such setbacks proved only temporary, however.

❖ THE GLORIOUS OLYMPIC GAMES

The decade's first, and only, Olympic Games were held in 1912 in Stockholm, Sweden. It was here that one of the most unfortunate and infamous incidents in modern-era Olympic history began unfolding. It started as a glorious feat: the victory, by Jim Thorpe (1881–1953), in both the decathlon and pentathlon. Furthermore, Thorpe's 8,412 decathlon points were a world's record. Upon presenting him with his gold medals, Sweden's King Gustav V (1858–1950) exclaimed, "Sir, you are the greatest athlete in the world." However, Thorpe's triumph was short-lived. A month after returning to the United States, the Amateur Athletic Union (AAU) charged him with professionalism when it was learned that he had briefly played semiprofessional baseball. The following year, he was stripped of his medals by the International Olympic Committee (IOC).

Otherwise, the 1912 games were the largest since the Olympics were revived in 1896. Close to twenty-five hundred athletes participated, representing twenty-eight nations. Sweden, the host country, garnered the most medals: twenty-four gold, twenty-four silver, and seventeen bronze, for a total of sixty-five. The United States earned sixty-one: twenty-three gold, nineteen silver, and nineteen bronze.

U.S. Lawn Tennis Association Singles Champions

Year	Male Winner	Female Winner
1910	William A. Larned	Hazel V. Hotchkiss
1911	William A. Larned	Hazel V. Hotchkiss
1912	Maurice E. McLoughlin	Mary K. Browne
1913	Maurice E. McLoughlin	Mary K. Browne
1914	Richard Norris Williams II	Mary K. Browne
1915	William M. Johnston	Molla Bjurstedt
1916	Richard Norris Williams	Molla Bjurstedt
1917	Robert L. Murray	Molla Bjurstedt
1918	Robert L. Murray	Molla Bjurstedt
1919	William M. Johnston	Hazel Hotchkiss Wightman

In addition to Thorpe, Americans triumphed in other track-and-field events. Ralph Craig (1889–1972), of the University of Michigan, won the 1200-meter and 200-meter races. Syracuse University's Charles Reidpath (1889–1975) captured the gold in the 400 meters, in an Olympic-record 48.2 seconds. James "Ted" Meredith (c.1895–1957), a Pennsylvania schoolboy, won the 800 meters in a world-record 1:51.9. Americans swept the medals in the pole vault, shot-put, and 110-meter high hurdles. (Throughout the decade, American track-and-field athletes consistently broke records and revolutionized their events. Among them were Howard P. Drew, an African American who was hailed as the "world's fastest human"; runners John Paul Jones, Abel Kiviat, and Norman Taber; high-jumper George Horine; pole-vaulter Marc Wright; and shot-putter Patrick J. McDonald.) Another noteworthy 1912 Olympian was Hawaii's Duke Kahanamoku (1890–1968), who won the 100-meter freestyle, the first of his five swimming medals spread over four Olympics.

That year the International Olympic Committee (IOC) expanded women's events, adding swimming and diving. Many opposed this change; in fact, James E. Sullivan (1862–1914), head of the Amateur Athletic Union (AAU), was against all women's sports. He refused to allow American women divers and swimmers to compete in the Olympics.

Since 1896, Germany had vigorously campaigned to host the Olympics. Upon learning that Berlin would be the likely site for the 1916 games, the Germans commenced construction of a thirty-four-thousand-seat stadium. However, the start of World War I effectively canceled the games.

❖ TENNIS

During the early part of the twentieth century, tennis, like golf, primarily was played by the well-to-do. While tennis courts mostly were found in private clubs, during the 1910s middle-class people began adopting the game. Additionally, tennis was one sport in which women competed as actively as men.

Early in the decade, Hazel V. Hotchkiss (1886–1974), who later became Hazel Hotchkiss Wightman, dominated the courts. She won several U.S. Lawn Tennis Association (USLTA) singles, doubles, and mixed

Tennis was one sport in which women, like May Sutton Bundy and Molla Bjurstedt, were able to compete as actively as men. Reproduced by permission of the United States Tennis Association.

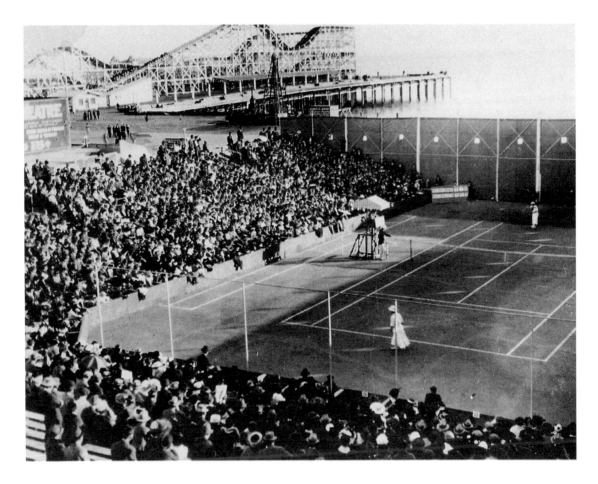

doubles championships. Her forceful forecourt play added an innovative dimension to women's tennis. From 1901 through 1911, William A. Larned (1872–1926) earned seven men's singles titles. Then Mary K. Browne (1891–1971) and Maurice E. McLoughlin (1890–1957), otherwise known as the "California Comet," each won several titles. McLoughlin in particular electrified the sport with his power serves, rushes to the net, deliberate volleying, and daring shots down the line. In mid-decade, William M. Johnston (1894–1946) succeeded McLoughlin as the game's top male player. He too played a power game, but his style was even more balanced and strategic. Through the end of the decade, Johnston won several singles and doubles titles.

In 1915, Norway's Molla Bjurstedt (1884–1959), a bronze-medal winner at the 1912 Olympics, became the initial foreigner to win the women's USLTA singles championship. It was the first of four straight titles. Her attempt at a fifth ended in defeat, when she lost to Hazel Hotchkiss Wightman in 1919.

 For More Information

BOOKS

Allen, Maury. *Big-Time Baseball: A Complete Record of the National Sport.* New York: Hart Publishing Company, 1978.

Bacho, Peter. *Boxing in Black and White.* New York: Henry Holt, 1999.

Carroll, Bob, Michael Gershman, David Neff, and John Thorn, eds. *Total Football II.* New York: HarperCollins, 1999.

Gilbert, Thomas. *Deadball: Major League Baseball Before Babe Ruth.* New York: Franklin Watts, 1996.

Heinz, W. C., and Nathan Ward, eds. *The Book of Boxing.* New York: Total Sports, 1999.

Heisler, John, and Knute Rockne. *Quotable Rockne.* Nashville, TN: TowleHouse Publishers, 2001.

Jacobs, William Jay. *They Shaped the Game: Ty Cobb, Babe Ruth, Jackie Robinson.* New York: Charles Scribner's Sons, 1994.

Jakoubek, Robert. *Jack Johnson.* New York: Chelsea House, 1990.

Kavanagh, Jack. *Shoeless Joe Jackson.* New York: Chelsea House, 1995.

Long, Barbara. *Jim Thorpe: Legendary Athlete.* Springfield, NJ: Enslow Publishers, 1997.

Ritter, Lawrence. *The Story of Baseball.* New York: Morrow Junior Books, 1999.

Sackler, Howard. *The Great White Hope.* New York: Dial Press, 1968.

Stewart, Mark. *Baseball: A History of the National Pastime.* New York: Franklin Watts, 1998.

Stewart, Mark. *Football: A History of the Gridiron Game.* New York: Franklin Watts, 1998.

Thorn, John, Pete Palmer, and Michael Gershman, eds. *Total Baseball, Seventh Edition.* Kingston, NY: Total Sports, 2001.

Wheeler, Robert. *Jim Thorpe: World's Greatest Athlete.* Norman: University of Oklahoma Press, 1985.

WEB SITES

Chicago Cubs History: 1910s. http://chicago.cubs.mlb.com/NASApp/mlb/chc/history/chc_history_timeline_article.jsp?article=3 (accessed on August 2, 2002).

Philadelphia Phillies History: 1910s. http://philadelphia.phillies.mlb.com/NASApp/mlb/phi/history/phi_history_timeline.jsp?period=3 (accessed on August 2, 2002).

Today in History. http://memory.loc.gov/ammem/today/dec10.html (accessed on August 2, 2002).

Where to Learn More

BOOKS

Adair, Gene. *Thomas Alva Edison: Inventing the Electric Age.* New York: Oxford University Press, 1996.

Allen, Maury. *Big-Time Baseball: A Complete Record of the National Sport.* New York: Hart Publishing Company, 1978.

Altman, Linda Jacobs. *The Decade that Roared: America During Prohibition.* New York: Twenty-First Century Books, 1997.

Andryszewski, Tricia. *Immigration: Newcomers and Their Impact on the United States.* Brookfield, CT: Millbrook Press, 1995.

Applebaum, Stanley, ed. *The New York Stage: Famous Productions in Photographs.* New York: Dover Publications, 1976

Archer, James. *They Had a Dream: The Civil Rights Struggle from Frederick Douglass to Marcus Garvey to Martin Luther King to Malcolm X.* New York: Viking, 1993.

Bacho, Peter. *Boxing in Black and White.* New York: Henry Holt, 1999.

Bachrach, Deborah. *The Importance of Margaret Sanger.* San Diego: Lucent Books, 1993.

Barr, Roger. *Radio: Wireless Sound.* San Diego: Lucent Books, 1994.

Bartoletti, Susan Campbell. *Growing Up in Coal Country.* Boston: Houghton Mifflin Juvenile, 1996.

Beardsley, John. *Henry James.* Broomall, PA: *Chelsea House,* 2001.

Beardsley, John. *Pablo Picasso.* New York: Harry N. Abrams, 1991.

Benowitz, Steven I. *Cancer.* Berkeley Heights, NJ: Enslow Publishers, 1999.

Where to Learn More

Bernstein, Jeremy. *Albert Einstein and the Frontiers of Physics*. New York: Oxford University Press, 1996.

Block, Irvin. *Neighbor to the World; the Story of Lillian Wald*. New York: Ty Crowell, 1969.

Bloom, Harold, ed. *Edith Wharton*. Philadelphia: Chelsea House, 2001.

Bloom, Harold, ed. *W.E.B. Du Bois*. Philadelphia: Chelsea House, 2001.

Blum, Daniel. *Great Stars of the American Stage*. New York: Grosset & Dunlap, 1952.

Blum, Daniel, enlarged by John Willis. *A Pictorial History of the American Theatre*, 6th ed. New York: Crown Publishers, 1986.

Blum, Daniel. *A Pictorial History of the Silent Screen*. New York: Putnam, 1953.

Bober, Natalie S. *A Restless Spirit: The Story of Robert Frost*. New York: Henry Holt, 1991.

Bolden, Tonya, ed. *33 Things Every Girl Should Know About Women's History: From Suffragettes to Skirt Lengths to the E.R.A.* New York: Crown Publishing, 2002.

Boulton, Alexander O. *Frank Lloyd Wright, Architect: An Illustrated Biography*. New York: Rizzoli, 1993.

Brown, Gene. *Conflict in Europe and the Great Depression: World War I*. New York: Twenty-First Century Books, 1993.

Bunting, Eve. *SOS Titanic*. San Diego: Harcourt Brace, 1996.

Carroll, Bob, Michael Gershman, David Neff, and John Thorn, eds. *Total Football II*. New York: HarperCollins, 1999.

Carter, David A. *George Santayana*. New York: Chelsea House, 1992.

Cohen, Daniel. *Yellow Journalism: Scandal, Sensationalism and Gossip in the Media*. Brookfield, CT: Twenty-First Century Books, 2000.

Cooper, Michael L. *Hell Fighters: African American Soldiers in World War I*. New York: Lodestar Books, 1997.

Davis, Frances A. *Frank Lloyd Wright: Maverick Architect*. Minneapolis: Lerner Publications, 1996.

Dolan, Edward F. *America in World War I*. Brookfield, CT: Millbrook Press, 1996.

Dolan, Terrance. *Probing Deep Space*. New York: Chelsea House, 1993.

Dowswell, Paul. *Weapons and Technology of World War I*. Chicago: Heinemann Library, 2002.

Ellis, Rex. *With a Banjo on My Knee: A Musical Journey from Slavery to Freedom*. New York: Franklin Watts, 2001.

Fox, Karen. *The Chain Reaction: Pioneers of Nuclear Science*. New York: Franklin Watts, 1998.

Gawne, Jonathan. *Over There!: The American Soldier in World War I*. Philadelphia, Chelsea House (reprint).

Gay, Kathlyn. *Who's Running the Nation? How Corporate Power Threatens Democracy*. New York: Franklin Watts, 1998.

Gilbert, Thomas. *Deadball: Major League Baseball Before Babe Ruth.* New York: Franklin Watts, 1996.

Gilbreth, Frank B., Jr., and Ernestine Gilbreth Carey. *Belles on Their Toes.* New York: Bantam, 1984 (reissue edition).

Gilbreth, Frank B., Jr., and Ernestine Gilbreth Carey. *Cheaper By the Dozen.* New York: Bantam, 1984 (reissue edition).

Gilbreth, Lillian Moller. *As I Remember: An Autobiography by Lillian Gilbreth.* Norcross, GA: Engineering & Management Press, 1998.

Goldenstern, Joyce. *Albert Einstein: Physicist and Genius.* Springfield, NJ: Enslow Publishers, 1995.

Gottfried, Ted. *The American Media.* New York: Franklin Watts, 1997.

Gourley, Catherine. *Good Girl Work: Sweatshops, and How Women Changed Their Role in the American Workforce.* Brookfield, CT: Millbrook Press, 1999.

Halliwell, Sarah, ed. *The Twentieth Century: Pre-1945 Artists, Writers, and Composers.* Austin, TX, Raintree/Steck-Vaughn, 1998

Haskins, James. *Separate, but Not Equal: The Dream and the Struggle.* New York: Scholastic, 1998.

Hatt, Christine. *World War I, 1914–1918.* New York: Franklin Watts, 2001.

Heinz, W. C., and Nathan Ward, eds. *The Book of Boxing.* New York: Total Sports, 1999.

Heisler, John, and Knute Rockne. *Quotable Rockne.* Nashville, TN: TowleHouse Publishers, 2001.

Hoag, Edwin, and Joy Hoag. *Masters of Modern Architecture: Frank Lloyd Wright, Le Corbusier, Mies van der Rohe, and Walter Gropius.* Indianapolis: Bobbs-Merrill, 1977.

Hyde, Margaret O. *Know About Tuberculosis.* New York: Walker & Company,1994.

Hyde, Margaret O., and Elizabeth H. Forsyth, MD. *Vaccinations: From Smallpox to Cancer.* New York: Franklin Watts, 2000.

Jacobs, William Jay. *They Shaped the Game: Ty Cobb, Babe Ruth, Jackie Robinson.* New York: Charles Scribner's Sons, 1994.

Jakoubek, Robert. *Jack Johnson.* New York: Chelsea House, 1990.

Janson, H. W., and Anthony F. Janson. *History of Art for Young People,* 5th ed. New York: Harry Abrams, 1997.

Jeffrey, Laura. *Great American Businesswomen.* Springfield, NJ: Enslow Publishers, 1996.

Katz, Ephraim. *The Film Encyclopedia,* 4th ed. New York: HarperResource, 2001.

Katz, William Loren. *Minorities in American History.* Vol. 4: *From the Progressive Era to the Great Depression, 1900–1929.* New York: Franklin Watts, 1974–75.

Kavanagh, Jack. *Shoeless Joe Jackson.* New York: Chelsea House, 1995.

Kent, Zachary. *World War I: The War to End All Wars.* Hillside, NJ: Enslow Publishers, 1994.

Kessler-Harris, Alice. *Women Have Always Worked: A Historical Overview.* New York: Feminist Press at the City University of New York, 1981.

Landau, Elaine. *Tuberculosis.* New York: Franklin Watts, 1995.

Laughlin, Rosemary. *John D. Rockefeller: Oil Baron and Philanthropist.* Greensboro, NC: Morgan Reynolds, 2001.

Lawler, Mary. *Marcus Garvey.* New York: Chelsea House, 1988.

Leach, William. *Edith Wharton.* New York: Chelsea House, 1987.

Lommel, Cookie. *Madame C. J. Walker.* Los Angeles: Melrose Square Publishing Company, 1993.

Long, Barbara. *Jim Thorpe: Legendary Athlete.* Springfield, NJ: Enslow Publishers, 1997.

Lucas, Eileen. *The Eighteenth and Twenty-First Amendments: Alcohol—Prohibition and Repeal.* Springfield, NJ: Enslow Publishers, 1998.

Lusane, Clarence. *The Struggle for Equal Education.* New York: Franklin Watts, 1992.

Macdonald, Fiona. *The World in the Time of Albert Einstein.* Parsippany, NJ: Dillon Press, 1998.

Maltin, Leonard, ed. *Leonard Maltin's Movie Encyclopedia.* New York: Dutton, 1994.

Matthews, Tom L. *Always Inventing: A Photobiography of Alexander Graham Bell.* Washington, DC: National Geographic Society, 1999.

Maurer, Richard. *Rocket! How a Toy Launched the Space Age.* New York: Crown Publishers, 1995.

McCarthy, Pat. *Henry Ford: Building Cars for Everyone.* Berkeley Heights, NJ: Enslow Publishers, 2002.

McClafferty, Carla Killough. *The Head Bone's Connected to the Neck Bone: The Weird, Wacky, and Wonderful X-Ray.* New York: Farrar Straus & Giroux, 2001.

McDaniel, Melissa. *W.E.B. Du Bois: Scholar and Civil Rights Activist.* New York: Franklin Watts, 1999.

Meltzer, Milton: *Bread and Roses: The Struggle of American Labor, 1865–1915.* New York, Knopf, 1967.

Muckenhoupt, Margaret. *Sigmund Freud: Explorer of the Unconscious.* New York: Oxford University Press, 1997.

O'Brien, Sharon, and Martin Duberman. *Willa Cather.* New York: Chelsea House, 1995.

O'Connell, Arthur J. *American Business in the twentieth Century.* San Mateo, CA: Bluewood Books, 1999.

Orgill, Roxane. *Shout, Sister, Shout! Ten Girl Singers Who Shaped a Century.* New York: Margaret McElderry, 2001.

Pasachoff, Naomi. *Alexander Graham Bell: Making Connections.* New York: Oxford University Press, 1996.

Pringle, Laurence P. *Chemical and Biological Warfare: The Cruelest Weapons.* Berkeley Heights, NJ: Enslow Publishers, 2000.

Randolph, Sallie G. *Woodrow Wilson.* New York: Walker & Company, 1992.

Reef, Catherine. *Sigmund Freud: Pioneer of the Mind.* New York: Clarion Books, 2001.

Rhym, Darren. *The NAACP.* Philadelphia: Chelsea House, 2001.

Ritter, Lawrence. *The Story of Baseball.* New York: Morrow Junior Books, 1999.

Rogers, James T. *Woodrow Wilson: Visionary for Peace.* New York: Facts on File, 1997.

Rubin, Susan Goldman. *Frank Lloyd Wright.* New York: Harry N. Abrams, 1994.

Sackler, Howard. *The Great White Hope.* New York: Dial Press, 1968.

Schroeder, Alan. *Charles Chaplin: The Beauty of Silence.* New York, Franklin Watts, 1997.

Severance, John B. *Einstein: Visionary Scientist.* New York: Clarion Books, 1999.

Siegel, Beatrice. *Lillian Wald of Henry Street.* New York: Macmillan, 1983.

Silverstein, Alvin, Virginia Silverstein, and Robert Silverstein. *Measles and Rubella.* Springfield, NJ: Enslow Publishers, 1997.

Silverstein, Alvin, Virginia Silverstein, and Robert Silverstein. *Tuberculosis.* Hillside, NJ: Enslow Publishers, 1994.

Simonds, Christopher. *The Model T Ford.* Englewood Cliffs, NJ: Silver Burdett Press, 1991.

Skurzynski, Gloria. *Rockbuster.* New York: Atheneum Books, 2001.

Slide, Anthony. *Early American Cinema.* New York: A.S. Barnes, 1970.

Sommerville, Donald. *World War I.* Austin, TX: Raintree/Steck-Vaughn, 1997.

Stewart, Gail. *1910s.* New York: Crestwood House, 1989.

Stewart, Gail. *Weapons of War.* San Diego: Lucent Books, 2001.

Stewart, Mark. *Baseball: A History of the National Pastime.* New York: Franklin Watts, 1998.

Stewart, Mark. *Football: A History of the Gridiron Game.* New York: Franklin Watts, 1998.

Stone, Tanya Lee. *The Progressive Era and World War I.* Austin, TX: Raintree/Steck-Vaughn, 2001.

Thorn, John, Pete Palmer, and Michael Gershman, eds. *Total Baseball,* 7th ed. Kingston, NY: Total Sports, 2001.

Topalian, Elyse. *Margaret Sanger.* New York: Franklin Watts, 1984.

Uschan, Michael V. *A Multicultural Portrait of World War I.* Tarrytown, NY: Benchmark Books, 1996.

Uschan, Michael V. *The 1910s.* San Diego, CA: Lucent Books, 1999.

Vaughan, William H. T. *Encyclopedia of Artists.* New York: Oxford University Press, 2000.

Weitzman, David. *Model T: How Henry Ford Built a Legend.* New York: Crown Publishers, 2002.

Wheeler, Robert. *Jim Thorpe: World's Greatest Athlete.* Norman: University of Oklahoma Press, 1985.

Whitelaw, Nancy. *Margaret Sanger: Every Child a Wanted Child.* New York: Dillon Press, 1994.

Williard, Charlotte. *Frank Lloyd Wright: American Architect.* New York: Macmillan, 1972.

Yancey, Diane. *Tuberculosis.* Brookfield, CT: Twenty-First Century Books, 2001.

Yannuzzi, Della A. *Madame C. J. Walker: Self-Made Businesswoman.* Berkeley Heights, NJ: Enslow Publishers, 2000.

WEB SITES

American Cultural History: The Twentieth Century, 1910–1919. http://www.nhm-ccd.cc.tx.us/contracts/lrc/kc/decade10.html (accessed on August 2, 2002).

The American Experience: Influenza 1918. http://www.pbs.org/wgbh/amex/influenza/ (accessed on August 2, 2002).

American Masters-D. W. Griffith. http://www.pbs.org/wnet/americanmasters/database/griffith_d.html (accessed on August 2, 2002).

Chicago Cubs History: 1910s. http://chicago.cubs.mlb.com/NASApp/mlb/chc/history/chc_history_timeline_article.jsp?article= 3 (accessed on August 2, 2002).

Children at Work, 1908–1912. http://www.ibiscom.com/hnintro.htm (accessed on August 2, 2002).

Colonel Edward House 1858–1938. http://www.pbs.org/wgbh/amex/wilson/peopleevents/p_house.html (accessed on August 2, 2002).

General Motors Corporation Corporate History: 1910s. http://www.gm.com/company/corp_info/history/gmhis1910.html (accessed on August 2, 2002).

The Great War and the Shaping of the Twentieth Century. http://www.pbs.org/greatwar/ (accessed on August 2, 2002).

Irving Berlin: In and Out of Time. http://www.kcmetro.cc.mo.us/pennvalley/biology/lewis/crosby/berlin.htm (accessed on August 2, 2002).

Joe Hill. http://www.pbs.org/joehill/ (accessed on August 2, 2002).

Nobel e-Museum. Edward Calvin Kendall-Biography. http://www.nobel.se/medicine/laureates/1950/kendall-bio.html (accessed on August 2, 2002).

Nobel e-Museum. Irving Langmuir-Biography. http://www.nobel.se/chemistry/laureates/1932/langmuir-bio.html (accessed on August 2, 2002).

Nobel e-Museum. John Raleigh Mott-Biography. http://www.nobel.se/peace/laureates/1946/mott-bio.html (accessed on August 2, 2002).

Nobel e-Museum. Theodore William Richards. http://www.nobel.se/chemistry/laureates/1914/richards-bio.html (accessed on August 2, 2002).

Noble e-Museum. Thomas Hunt Morgan-Biography. http://www.nobel.se/medicine/laureates/1933/morgan-bio.html (accessed on August 2, 2002).

Person of the Century: Albert Einstein. http://www.time.com/time/time100/poc/home.html (accessed on August 2, 2002).

Philadelphia Phillies History: 1910s. http://philadelphia.phillies.mlb.com/NASApp/mlb/phi/history/phi_history_timeline.jsp?period=3 (accessed on August 2, 2002).

Robert Goddard. http://www.time.com/time/time100/scientist/profile/goddard.html (accessed on August 2, 2002).

Samuel Gompers. http://www.pbs.org/joehill/faces/gompers.html (accessed on August 2, 2002).

Today in History. http://memory.loc.gov/ammem/today/dec10.html (accessed on August 2, 2002).

The Two Nations of Black America. http://www.pbs.org/wgbh/pages/frontline/shows/race/etc/road.html (accessed on August 2, 2002).

U.S. National Archives and Records Administration. The Constitution: The 19th Amendment. http://www.archives.gov/exhibit_hall/charters_of_freedom/constitution/19th_amendment.html (accessed on August 2, 2002).

The White House. Woodrow Wilson. http://www.whitehouse.gov/history/presidents/ww28.html (accessed on August 2, 2002).

Index